AF422994

Until I read Elliot Glicksman's

"So far so good" we were best friends. His book is such a delightful, charming, clever, breezy memoir of his rich, full and accomplished life I had to put it down. What does a professional published writer like myself do when you find your "best friend" is a superior author, the better writer? As well as being multitalented? He plays the Ukelele for God's sake. It's humiliating and stunning. And this is just this shmuck's first book.

Obeying my wife's order to swallow my petty envy of my alleged best friend I will grudgingly concede "So far so good" was warm, surprising, engaging, laugh out loud funny, often poignant and entirely memorable. In every chapter we hear the gifted author's unique self-deprecating voice. On every page we meet an uncommonly kind and optimistic personal philosophy weaving through a mesmerizing collection of life stories, anecdotes and vignettes that will resonate with you.

It was a joy to spend an entire day with this book. Glicksman is a master of observational humor, pathos and resilient mirth. I felt I was laughing and crying my way through the creative framework for a one man play that I did not want to end. Bravo, buddy. You got a standing ovation from me, your "friend", "the writer". I'm still jealous. Putz.

David Fitzsimmons
"Arizona's Progressive Voice"
https://davidwfitzsimmons.substack.com/
fitztooner@outlook.com
Tucson, Arizona

You know that friend who always

has something funny to say. And how you think if you could just write down the conversation and edit out the unfunny parts, you'd be left with pure comic gold.

Well, this is not that book.

Elliot Glicksman did not edit out all the unfunny parts and it turns out that's OK because when I sat down to read "So Far, So Good," I heard Elliot's voice. It's an entertaining voice even when it's not 100-percent funny.

Don't get me wrong: This book is funny. The first four chapters read like a stand-up routine, which is totally appropriate for a writer who is, in fact, a stand-up comedian.

But he's more than that, as you'll find out when he settles in to tell his story. He's a husband and father and grandfather and the kind of friend you'd like to have in your corner when things get dicey. He's also an attorney who spent his career helping people who had been grievously injured find some justice.

But don't take my words for it. Read his. There are only 51,735 of them. He counted.

You'll find out why Elliot's family and friends tolerate his humor, even when it's at their expense. It's because there is a nice guy behind the jokes. And there is a nice story between them.

Tom Beal, former writer, columnist and editor
Arizona Daily Star

So Far, So Good

Answers to Questions
I Should Have Been Asked

a quasi-humorous and partly truthful memoir by
Elliot Glicksman

A3D Impressions
Tucson | Minneapolis

First A3D Impressions Edition May 2023
Publisher's Cataloging-in-Publication data

Names: Glicksman, Elliot, author.
Title: So far , so good : answers to questions I should have been asked / a quasi-humorous and
partly truthful memoir by Elliot Glicksman.
Description: Tucson, AZ; Minneapolis, MN: A3D Impressions, 2023.
Identifiers: LCCN: 2023940715 | ISBN: 979-8-9864049-9-8 (paperback) | 978-1-7320677-4-5
(ebook)
Subjects: LCSH: Glicksman, Elliot. | Comedians--United States--Biography. | Lawyers--Biography.
| Humorous stories. | BISAC: BIOGRAPHY & AUTOBIOGRAPHY / Personal Memoirs |
BIOGRAPHY & AUTOBIOGRAPHY / Entertainment & Performing Arts | BIOGRAPHY &
AUTOBIOGRAPHY / Lawyers & Judges | HUMOR / Form / Essays
Classification: LCC PN2287 .G55 2023 | DDC 792.2/092--dc23

This is a work of non-fiction. However, certain names have been changed to protect the
privacy of persons referenced in this work.

Cover and book design: Donn Poll

CONTENTS

Chapter		Page
1	Are You Bothered by Any Bedding, Holidays, or Amendments to the Constitution?	1
2	What It's Like To Become a Father?	7
3	Do You Have Any Strong Feelings about Any Welsh Singers?	12
4	Does Heaven Exist?	17
5	Should This Have Been the First Chapter?	21
6	How Did Your Parents Choose Your Name?	27
7	What Religion are You?	33
8	What Differences Have You Observed between Men and Women?	40
9	What Were Your Most Humiliating Life Experiences?	46
10	What Are Some of the Most Important Things You've Learned?	51
11	Can You Explain Aging?	55
12	What Was Your Favorite Trip?	60
13	Do You Have Any Family Stories to Share?	71
14	Do You Keep in Touch with Many High School Friends?	75
15	What Was Your First Job?	83
16	What Were Your College Years Like?	90
17	Why Did You Move to Tucson?	99
18	What Was the Toughest Decision You've Had to Make?	104
19	What Happened to Bob and Bob?	117
20	Did You Keep a Journal After Your Granddaughter Mackenzie was Born?	128
21	Do You Have Any Child-Raising Tips?	136
22	Would It Be Boring to Read about Your Law Practice?	142
23	Why So Far, So Good for the Title?	153
	Afterword	160

CHAPTER 1

Are You Bothered by Any Bedding, Holidays, or Amendments to the Constitution?

I'm so glad to answer this question as I'm upset with pillows, holidays, and the Second Amendment to the Constitution. When I was a boy, I had *one* pillow on my bed. My parents shared a bed. They had two pillows. My wife Lorraine and I share a bed, at least until she reads this, and there are fifteen pillows on my bed. Fifteen! And a teddy bear.

There's an order in which the pillows are to be placed on our bed. I took a picture of the bed after she made it so I could study it while she was out of town. I made a schematic of Mount Pillow-monjaro and memorized it. While she was gone, it was a whole lot easier to just move a few pillows on my side of the bed, pull down the covers, and sleep on the very edge of the bed so as not to disturb the dozen other perfectly placed pillows ... or the teddy bear.

And it isn't just the proper pillow placement on the bed that's required. Apparently, pillow etiquette has rigid

1

removal requirements for said pillows on our bedroom floor and chair. Like pillow Jenga. Remove one without care and the whole tower of pillows collapses. I recently committed the offense of having smooshed one of the small rectangular pillows under a large square pillow. You know the pillows I mean: the ones that are big enough to smother a yak. I don't really understand how a pillow can smoosh anything. It's a pillow, not a microwave. A helium balloon weighs more. Obviously, if I'd put a microwave on a rectangular pillow, that would be indefensible, and there'd be no explaining why I brought a microwave into the bedroom. And the little rectangular pillow would definitely be smooshed. But a bigger pillow on a smaller pillow? Really?

**Perfectly placed piles to
prevent prolonged pressing
of petite pillows**

That was the final straw for me. I was done. Lorraine was out shopping for more pillows when I thought, *Pillow protocol be damned!* Two weeks ago, I began just tossing the pillows off the bed and letting them land wherever—on top of each other, next to each other. Who cares? I'm the man of the house, and I'll place the pillows wherever I want. What was the pillow policewoman going to do about it?

I miss having sex. Thank God I still have my teddy bear.

This whole pillow thing is a relatively new phenomenon in my marriage. But the bed has always been an issue. Lorraine likes a neatly made bed, and every morning she makes it. For many years, I could not lie in the bed after it was made out of Lorraine's concern that someone would come by and see—horrors—our rumpled comforter.

Lorraine has a protocol whenever company comes over. And why do we call it *company*? It's not like General Mills is coming for dinner. (Is there even a General Mills, and did he serve in Hungary?) When guests come over—military, civilian, whoever—Lorraine insists that the house look as though no one has ever lived there. Like the guests are the first people to have ever set foot in a model home. By the way, I was able to lie on the bed after it was made once we got our dog, Miles. Miles always jumped on the bed. At that point, it seemed unfair, even to Lorraine, that Miles was allowed on the bed when I wasn't. And I don't shed nearly as much as he does.

So back to having fifteen pillows when all my life I was perfectly content with one. How did it get to this point? Did Martha Stewart walk into a bedroom and say, "Hey, wait just a doggone minute. There's way too much of that comforter showing!" Did the pillow push begin because of a surplus of down after people started wearing fiber-fill jackets? I suspect it was a consortium of pillow manufacturers at a conference sitting around a table thinking: "We're going to go broke if this one pillow per bed situation continues. We need to create a demand for pillows the same way Hallmark invented bullshit holidays to sell more cards."

Growing up, I don't recall ever having seen a Secretaries Day (more recently, Administrative Professionals Day) on my calendar. Do we really need to celebrate March 14, National Potato Chip Day, or April 29, National Shrimp Scampi Day? We've created so many holidays that many fall on the same day. In 2019, January 13 was Korean American Day, National Sticker Day, National Rubber Ducky Day,

National Peach Melba Day, Stephen Foster Memorial Day, and National Sunday Supper Day. And you can bet Hallmark had the perfect card to celebrate National Sunday Supper Day and all the rest: "Why sell one card with all six holidays on it when American consumers will pay for six separate cards?"

With all those festivities, I may not be in any kind of shape to celebrate National Hot Pastrami Sandwich Day on January 14. There's no governing body creating these days. I'm sure it's just Hallmark. Can I proclaim, "Hey, today is Elliot Glicksman Day"? No. But if I promised to buy one thousand Elliot Glicksman Day greeting cards, I'm guessing I could make it happen. And then guess what? Every day is going to be Elliot Glicksman Day. I'll differentiate the days. One day will be Elliot Glicksman Rode His Bike Day, and the next day could be Elliot Glicksman Should Have a Martini Day.

But back to the pillows. Can you imagine the lightbulb going on when someone said, "Hey, if everyone had two pillows instead of one, we could double our profits."

Then the next person yelled, "What if we could get three pillows per bed?"

"Four," shouted another. Soon a frenzy of pillow makers was wondering aloud, "Five? Would people really ever put five pillows on a bed?"

"How would we do that?"

And then someone yelled out, "I know! Call Martha Stewart; tell her we'll give her a cut of the profits if she begins pillow shaming her friends on TV."

"Pillow shaming?"

"Yeah, you know. In one episode, Martha goes to a friend's house in the Hamptons, shakes her head, and says, 'That's a sad-looking one-pillow bed you have there." Or, "Your bed. It looks so naked with that one lonely pillow." Or she could say, "Oh, your bed reminds me of when I was in prison, and we could only have one pillow on our bed." That sort of thing.

It's all about marketing. Creating a need. The NRA, which is really an arm of the gun-manufacturing industry, uses creative marketing to sell guns. Their marketing approach uses basic human emotion and an appeal to the reptilian part of the brain: survival. Gun sales are marketed by weaponizing fear and concern for the safety of your family: more guns would make you safer, protect you. It was genius. They sold bumper stickers that read: "Guns, Yes! Crime, No!" A slogan that was clever. A slogan that was catchy. And a slogan that ignored reality. I've got one for you. "Cigarettes, Yes! Cancer, No!"

Now we need guns in every room of our house, loaded and ready to shoot any marauding intruders. I know a guy who has a gun in his bedroom. He says it makes him feel safer. Manlier. Whatever. His wife tells me he shoots blanks.

"We need to be armed on the street to defend the innocent." "Police should have no problem telling the armed bad guy from the good guy with the gun." "We need guns in schools, churches, movie theaters, and concert stadiums. More guns is the only way to make us safe." If only they'd had people trained to use guns at the Fort Hood military base in 2014 when Ivan Lopez killed four and wounded 14, I'm sure someone could have prevented it. Makes you want to cover your head with a pillow made out of Kevlar.

I've heard the arguments against gun safety measures: "If you have a law restricting gun ownership, criminals won't obey the law." That may be true. But if that's the case, why have laws prohibiting murder and rape? Murderers and rapists won't obey the law. The bottom line? Gun control will adversely affect the gun-manufacturing industry.

Then there's the "violation of my Second Amendment rights" argument. The Second Amendment is apparently the number-one, greatest, best, most awesome amendment in the Bill of Rights. This is surprising since it is, after all, the *Second* Amendment. Restrictions on all the other amendments are allowed. The First Amendment says you can't make any law "abridging the freedom of speech," but the law can prohibit someone from yelling, "Fire!" in a crowded theater.

The Fourth Amendment prohibits searches without a warrant, but there's an exception for emergencies like having to break into a home to save someone's life. Like the other night when Lorraine had me cornered with a decorator pillow. I would have been dead if my mom hadn't broken in through the bathroom window to save me.

Somehow, the Second Amendment has been given the preeminent place among gun owners and manufacturers. The Second Amendment says the right to bear arms "shall not be infringed." The argument is that gun-safety rules "infringe" and punish a law-abiding, God-fearing citizen of the United States by preventing them from owning arms like a nuclear rocket launcher just because a terrorist might misuse it.

It's discouraging to try to take on the NRA and their fear-mongering. It's much easier to fight the pillow wars. There is no constitutional amendment that pillow profiteers can hide behind. Guys, we can win the pillow war. We just have to go without sex. Hang on to your teddy bear.

CHAPTER 2

What's it Like
To Become a Father?

You never know how wonderful life can be until you have children. And then it's too late. I'm kidding. I have two beautiful children. The third one not so much. Long before our child was born, Lorraine and I attended birthing classes. On the first day of class, we were shown movies. In school, movies were a sure sign the teacher was hungover. But watching films in Lamaze class just made me think this whole kid thing may have been a mistake.

We were told the movies would show us the beauty and miracle of childbirth. What we saw were horror flicks to rival Stephen King or Ridley Scott. The movies had sweet-sounding names like *Natural Childbirth: Labors of Love.* But no saccharin title changes the fact that *Caesarians: A Slice of Life* was strikingly similar to a terrifying scene from *Alien.* I longed for the days I'd seen on the classic film channel, when guys just paced the waiting room with a bunch of cigars.

I understood why these movies were shown after a woman was pregnant. Had they been shown in the fifth grade, there would be no pregnancies and probably very little sex. Other than scaring the crap out of you, the main purpose of having couples attend birthing class is to make the guy feel shitty about putting his wife in this horrible situation and to find something for him to do during the birthing process so he doesn't just hang out in the waiting room with a bunch of guys lamenting that they were no longer allowed to smoke cigars in a hospital.

The Lamaze teacher explained alternative ways of giving birth, like in a bathtub, and ways to deal with pain, including an epidural block. I suggested Lorraine not take any of the drugs offered during childbirth so we could save them until our kid was a teenager and sedatives were really needed.

The reality is that from the time of conception until the child is born, guys are worthless. Your Lamaze instructor will try to get guys interested. She'll use sports metaphors. She may even call you "Coach" and say you're an important part of the "team." Trying to make sperm donors feel like participants in the miracle of birth is like telling the guy that hands towels to basketball players that his three-point basket won the game. But I get it. If your wife has to go through the misery of passing a football-sized human out of her vagina, you can damn well share some of the horror of watching this catastrophe unfold.

Like real coaches, you don't play the game. You're on the sidelines. During the birthing process, one of your few responsibilities might be to give your wife ice chips, which I suppose to a pregnant woman is like Gatorade. Frankly, this is not even what a real coach does. A real coach comes up with a game plan. Like the guy who passes out towels, the person who passes out Gatorade to the players is usually an intern, the nonathletic guy who wants to feel like he's part of the team but is just a guy whose most important job is to collect and wash soiled uniforms. But coach sounds way cooler and more important than intern and you can't be called an intern in the hospital because that's what they call real doctors who actually do something during the birth.

But as the coach, you do have one important job. When

your wife is dilated to 10 inches or whatever size she's supposed to be, you start screaming in her face, "Push! Push!" Not much of a coaching job as it doesn't require a whole lot of in-game strategy, but it's important because if you start yelling it prematurely and she starts pushing too soon, she can actually blow her eyeballs right out of the socket. That's true. It was in the movie.

I was definitely ready to coach my wife in labor. In the delivery room, I yelled, "Push!" She pushed, and out came our mucus-covered, face-smooshed son. Then get this: The doctor looked at me and asked, "Cut the cord?" To which I responded, "No friggin' way! And when I'm doing that, you'd be doing what? Telling jokes at the nurse's station?" "No, really," he insisted, waving what looked like garden shears in my face. So now I'm in the game. I'm a player. I'm going to cut the cord. Suddenly, I'm terrified. This is big. This is "at the free-throw line, down by one, with time expired, and you have two free throws" big. "Bottom of the ninth, bases loaded, down by a run in game seven of the World Series" big. I'm nervous. I step out. I have visions of cutting the cord, my kid deflating like a balloon and flying around the room. Psssst.

For whatever it's worth, there's no dictionary word for the sound of air rushing out of a balloon. At least until I submit psssst. You may think there's already a "psssst" out there, but you'd be wrong. Psst is an exclamation meaning "used to get someone's attention," according to the Merriam-Webster online dictionary. An online urban dictionary has a three-S pssst as "loud remark used to grab everybody's attention before telling someone's secret." I briefly considered using pfft for the balloon sound, but that same dictionary defined pfft as "an expression of a lack of interest in another person's comment or to look down on another."

So the doctor tells me to cut the cord. And all these thoughts run through my head. What if I cut too high and leave too much on, and my son looks like he has a second penis growing out of his stomach? I didn't care if he had an innie or even a little outie, but please don't leave him with a pumpkin stem. And then I just did it. Snip. And it was perfect.

But here's the secret the doctors don't tell you before you cut. Spoiler alert: You really can't screw it up. The part you leave attached to the belly button falls off in a few days. So it doesn't matter where you cut. You can leave a long cord and use it as a handle if you want. Or take a picture of your son's shadow and tell your friends that you and your wife are creating a master race of porn stars.

So that's pretty much all there is to the birth itself. Say "push" really loud while you're coaching, snip the cord wherever you want, and that's it. So you can imagine the pride I had in the surgical precision with which I cut the cord. Not only did I ask the doctor if she'd ever seen such a perfect cut—and on my first try, no less—but I went on to explain exactly how I'd done it and how I lined up the scissor blade with the umbilical cord. I offered to do an in-service for interns at the hospital in the operating theater. The doctor gave me a curt, "No, thanks. I think we have it covered" and left the room.

To recap: Despite all the stuff they tell you about your role in the birthing process, you don't do anything. Moms want you in the room because they don't think it's fair for them to have to have the baby while you're in the waiting room watching football, hanging out, and holding a bunch of unlit cigars with other soon-to-be dads. Honestly, it's very cool to be in the room when your kid is born. But don't let anyone scare you about the birthing process. I went through it twice. It's no biggie.

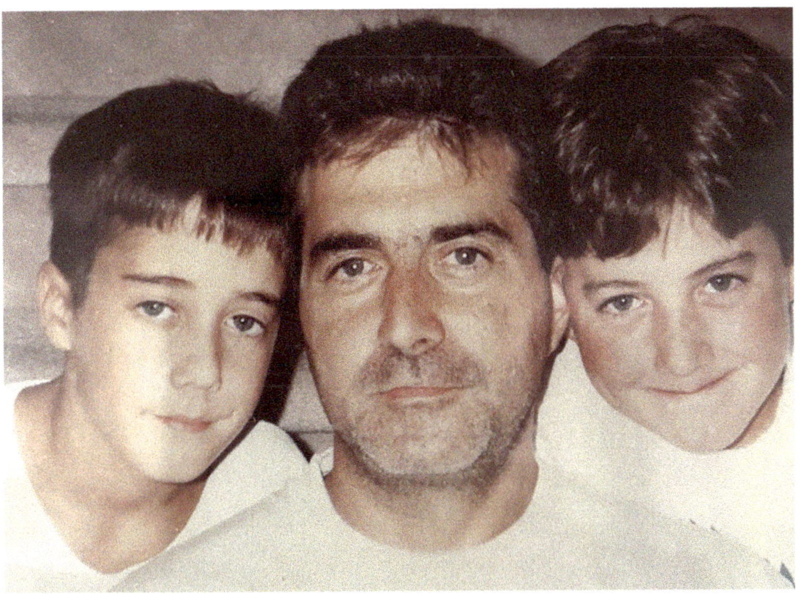

Zach and Ben who I successfully coached from their mother's womb

CHAPTER 3

Do You Have Any Strong Feelings about Any Welsh Singers?

Yes, I have strong feelings about a singer from Wales. I hate Tom Jones. Hate him. I should probably take a moment to explain why. I'm sometimes nearly crippled by insecurity. My insecurities are overwhelming. "I feel like everyone is staring and laughing at me," I told my therapist.

"Maybe you shouldn't be doing standup comedy. And, trust me, I've seen your act; the audience is only staring," he responded, turning his dog-eared pages of Counseling for Dummies. But that's not what I'm talking about. Yes, I am insecure on stage. I wish they wouldn't introduce me as a comedian. I'd prefer the emcee introduce me as a humorist to lower audience expectations. Or a philosopher.

But it's not just onstage. I feel like people can tell I'm faking being grown up. Everyone else seems more together than me, at least from the looks of their Facebook posts. I pretend to know what I'm doing in almost every aspect of my life. When I take my car to a mechanic, I'm sure they know that I know nothing about cars. So I fake it. After not shaving for a few days, I go into the "shop." To more fully look like a "car guy," I wear a baseball cap and chew gum, even though I've never played baseball and can't blow a bubble. Bubba looks up from under the hood and says, "the intake manifold."

I nod, spit out my gum while trying to blow a bubble, and sigh. "Yep, yep, yep ... that's what I figured. Either the intake manifold or the upholstery." And he stares. And I know he knows I'm faking it.

Insecurity doesn't make me think over things. It makes me overthink things. When someone texts me, should I respond right away? If I do, will they think I don't have a life and that I just sit around waiting for someone to text me? But if I wait to respond, will they think I'm really full of myself for not responding sooner? What's the right length? What's the right circumference? That's a different issue. Does everyone fake it till they make it? Not my wife, Lorraine. I'm positive she fakes it till I make it. Or maybe she doesn't. I'm so insecure about my sexual prowess that when I'm in bed with her, I fantasize *I'm* someone else.

My insecurity stems from my height or lack thereof. I could write a whole chapter on this. See chapter 5. These insecurities are why I hate Tom Jones, the Welsh singer. Not *Tom Jones*, the movie with Albert Finney, which was named the 51st best British film by the British Film Academy in 1999. (If I'm not mistaken at number 52 for best British films of all time was a 1958 documentary of Queen Elizabeth eating soup.) No, I hate Tom Jones the singer, whom Lorraine has seen in concert a dozen times over the last 50 years.

If that sounds like a short, insecure, jealous guy, it's only because I'm a short, insecure, jealous guy. But most short, insecure, jealous guys just worry about things in the realm of the possible, like their wife being swept off her feet by a tall, handsome ex-boyfriend, a coworker, or even a casual acquaintance. Don't get me wrong. I worry about those things too. But my insecurities extend to going to a concert with my wife and worrying she'll leave with the band.

And that's why I hate Tom Jones. Throughout our 30-

plus years of marriage, one thing, and only one thing, has really been constant. Not our love or support of one another, or our shared dislike of green olives and Pauly Shore, or even our kids. Nope. The one constant in our lives has been Tom Jones. In the seven Tom Jones concerts I've attended, when Tom comes onstage, Lorraine makes little moaning noises. Little aaahs or oooohs. Other than at these concerts, I've never heard these sounds. And despite my best efforts, I've certainly never been able to elicit them.

"Really?" you say. "You're really worried that from up on the stage, Tom Jones would summon her and that she'd saunter up, mesmerized, and never return?" It would be silly and juvenile to waste time worrying about something like that. Is it silly to worry because, at the last Las Vegas show we attended, she took an extremely long trip to the bathroom while George Wallace was performing his opening act?

Why should I feel insecure? Just because Lorraine carries a picture of Tom Jones in her purse? Doesn't everyone? If you're thinking maybe the purse maker gives TJ's picture away with every wallet, like the photos of good-looking couples that come in picture frames. No, sir. Lorraine has a picture of Tom Jones that she cut out of a local paper five years ago. Why should I worry? Maybe the lipstick smears on the picture were there when she cut it out. She tells me I'm crazy to be jealous of Tom Jones. But she doesn't have a picture of me in her purse, five years old or otherwise. Or our children. We have three. (Without bragging, two of them could really be in those picture frames they sell. The third, not so much.)

From the time they were old enough to understand, I calmly explained to our children that their mom and dad love each other, but if Tom Jones ever comes to the door, that's it. Mom is gone. Lorraine would shake her head and tell me I was being ridiculous. But I'm positive she said that only because she never thought he'd come. Believe me, if he showed up, the kids and I would be getting postcards from Vegas.

I've been to seven Tom Jones concerts. You could easily have recognized me as the only guy in the front row, the one picking women's underwear off the back of his neck. I just throw the panties up on the stage after I'm sure they're not Lorraine's. My last Tom Jones concert was on May 7, 2014, at the Rialto Theatre in Tucson. Tom was 74. He and his fans have aged. The show looked like an AARP conference. After getting plucked twice, a woman made her way to the front row, fabric clutched tightly in her bony fingers. She looked like she'd spent the afternoon making popsicle-stick log cabins at an assisted living facility. Her intentions were obvious. Leaning over her walker, I jokingly asked toothless Eleanor Roosevelt whether she'd toss up a thong or briefs. She said, "Depends."

I shouldn't hate Tom. There are benefits to my wife's 40-year obsession with TJ. In some ways, he's helped our love life. In 1992, for our anniversary, I surprised Lorraine with a flight to Las Vegas to see him. Not the George Wallace restroom trip. There I was in the front row, watching my wife sitting on the edge of her seat. And hearing her make those little moaning sounds again.

Well, this time, after the concert, I took advantage of TJ's performance—or, as I call it, foreplay. I took Lorraine up to our room, dimmed the lights, lit a candle, and put on a CD of some Tom Jones love songs. Then to recreate the erotic, hot, sweaty moments and perhaps elicit those moaning sounds that my wife uttered only minutes earlier, I slipped on a pair of skintight black leather pants. Finally, to complete the look, I took a potato and I ... well, I just stuck it—I'm guessing some of you are way ahead of me here—I stuck it down my pants. Unfortunately, this did not enhance the mood. Not at all. I probably should have stuck it down the front. There was no soft moaning, no ooohs or aaahs. Honestly, I didn't mind that so much. It was her uncontrolled laughter that really bugged me.

At a Tom Jones concert in Tucson, a local radio station set up a meet and greet before the concert. I was friendly with a DJ and arranged for Lorraine to get backstage to shake his hand and get a picture with him. When she walked out the stage door toward our seats, she was beaming. Really glowing. With growing anticipation as she got ever closer, I waited for her to look into my eyes, throw her arms around me, and say something like, "You are a wonderful husband," or "God, I'm lucky as hell to have you," or "I'm going to ride you like a pony tonight." Nope, her first words were "He's taller than you." Really. Bingo!

Granted, I'm a short guy. But now I have to hear that Tom, who, at 74, is better-looking than me and has an incredible singing voice, is also taller than me. "I looked, and he wasn't wearing big heels," she continued. Thanks again. So Tom Jones is taller than me. Big deal. Big effin' deal. I hate Tom Jones.

Lorraine and Tom Jones at his Tucson concert

CHAPTER 4

Does Heaven Exist?

I'm not working. Being retired, I have time to contemplate this frequently asked question. But before answering whether heaven exists, let's discuss living. My dad says that life is like a roll of toilet paper: the closer you get to the end, the faster it goes. If that's the case, hopefully I've got a lot of three-ply left. I probably do as I think I've heard people say, "That Elliot, he's full of sheets". I'm almost positive that's what they were saying. Maybe I don't feel like I'm near the end of the roll because my parents are both still alive. I haven't even reached the front of the death line yet. Each day I'm closer to the front of the line than the day before, but there's still a buffer between me and the grim reaper. That might be why I don't spend a lot of time thinking about death.

Since I'm not working, I could start contemplating this age-old question. I'm retired. Retirement means time to read a morning newspaper, get excited about rain totals, and think about death. My first thought is that I'm glad we're all in this life together. It would suck to be the only one who was going to die. Not that I fear death. I've watched a Steven Seagal movie marathon. I've invested in New Coke, and I've attended a four-year-old's birthday party at Little Joey's Jumping Castle and Face Paint Emporium. Clearly, there are things worse than death.

Scientists, philosophers, and theologians have spent

lifetimes contemplating what happens after you die. People have pondered the question of the hereafter as long as there have been people. If the most brilliant minds haven't been able to figure it out, it seems like a colossal waste of time for me to spend a moment trying. I'll know the answer when I die. Until then, I don't worry about it. That having been said, I've heard some pretty interesting ideas about the afterlife.

One common belief is that when you die, you go to heaven and see dead relatives. In heaven, your dead relatives are waiting for you? Let's hope not. I spent a lifetime trying to avoid these people. Really? Heaven cannot be having to listen to my aunt Sadie ask me why I never called my cousin Kenny when I was in Wisconsin in 1995? If that were heaven for me, it would have to be hell for my relatives. Let me explain.

You're taught if you're nice, you go to heaven. Okay, but if heaven's the reward, once you've entered the pearly gates, there's no further incentive to be nice. Why bother? You made it! You're in heaven. You've been good. So I don't have to be nice to my aunt Sadie once I'm in heaven. She falls down, I'm not helping her up. Why should I? I tripped her. And I certainly don't have to be nice when my aunt Sadie guilt trips me for not calling Cousin Kenny when I was in Wisconsin.

"You were in Sheboygan for a week, and you couldn't call your cousin Kenny?"

"Aunt Sadie. First, it was an afternoon in Sheboygan. It just felt like a week. Second, I hate Cousin Kenny even more than I hate Sheboygan. And third, I never liked your meatloaf. It sucked. Your meatloaf made me want to puke all over Sheboygan."

Heaven, should it exist, has to be better than a place where dead Glicksmans are waiting to ambush me. Heaven should be a wondrous place where I see that the toilet paper roll is empty before I ever sit down, a place where the Starbucks barista correctly spells *Elliot*, and a place where I can have sex twice in one month.

Some Christians believe you don't have to be good to get to heaven. They believe entrance to the hereafter doesn't need a lifetime of good works. As long as you repent and accept Jesus before you die, these Christians believe, you go to heaven. I don't know if they're right or wrong but the pitch is that it's never too late. Repent and accept Jesus, and you're in. That sounds all well and good, but clearly this sucks if you've spent your entire life doing good deeds, and you're in heaven's cafeteria eating next to Johnny-come-lately repentant Jeffrey Dahmer. "Yeah, I'm sure you're really sorry Mr. Dahmer, but can you get your fork away from my leg?"

Of course, the downside to the "just accept Jesus and you go to heaven" mantra is the belief that Jesus is not only *a* way in; it's the only way. Hindus? Out. Buddhists? Out. Muslims, Jews, and atheists? Do you really even need to ask? No matter how good you were or how kind in your lifetime, at this exclusive club, if you don't know Jesus, you're stuck behind the rope line. So if accepting Jesus puts me in heaven's buffet line behind repentant Hitler, I'll take my chances in Hell's Kitchen with Moses, Buddha, and Gandhi. And I'm guessing Gandhi will give me his dessert.

As we age, it's natural for people to start thinking about death. They're running out of toilet paper. The older they get, the more they worry. Some folks start hedging their bets and find religion, or return to the religion of their youth. They start studying the Bible like they're cramming for finals. I don't know about other religions, but temples are full of old Jews. Old Jews and little kids. Parents bring their little kids to temples and don't go back again until they're 80. That's what synagogue congregations are: pediatric and geriatric Jews.

But I can't waste my time worrying about death. I'll leave it to the philosophers, theologians, and scientists to devote their lives to figuring out what happens when we die. I could do that too, but that sort of effort seems an awful lot like work. And, as you'll recall, I'm not working.

Me and Mahatma Gandhi having lunch in hell

CHAPTER 5

Should This Have Been the First Chapter?

I wrote this book to answer some questions that should have been asked, tell some stories, and share some thoughts. I planned to start this book with an introduction or prologue, which comes before the first chapter the way boys come before girls. In the dictionary. But I kept writing and rewriting the introduction so much that I feared the last glacier would melt and Donald Trump would concede the 2020 election before it was finished. So I wrote the previous chapters first. Now my introduction is chapter 5.

This could never have been a prologue for many reasons, not the least of which is prologue suggests something written by a pro. There's nothing "pro" about my writing. The fact you've read this far suggests it's more like a con. Someone who's a pro has an agent, an editor and, most importantly, readers. Being a pro means you're someone who gets paid. So if a prologue is something written by a pro, this isn't it. I'm not being modest, although I do have a lot to be modest about.

Perhaps the pro in prologue has nothing to do with being paid. As a young lawyer, I mistakenly agreed to take three pro bono cases based on my belief these paid well because a "pro" got paid, and bono was probably Latin for good. Turned out I was providing free legal services to three schmucks who couldn't afford a lawyer. In my defense, I never attended Catholic school or traveled to Latin America, so I ought to be forgiven for not reading or speaking the language.

Maybe pro in this instance also has nothing to do with compensation. Just like a dialogue is a conversation between two people, and a monologue is one person talking, maybe a prologue is someone strongly in favor of talking. In any event, under any definition of the word, this isn't a prologue, more like an amateurlogue.

A prologue, an introduction, or, in this case, an amateurlogue is at the beginning of a book. As we've discussed, this isn't the beginning, and it may not be a book. I've been told that a book must have 50,000 words at a minimum. And I'm pretty sure that prologues aren't even included in the word count. Pages in a prologue don't even have numbers except occasionally little, tiny Roman numerals. (Note to self: If I ever hope to approach 50,000 words, from now on stay away from contractions like "aren't" and use "are not"—two words that way. Can't is okay because cannot is still just one word.)

I have no delusions about this becoming a book. Fifty thousand words seems insurmountable. And I'm not going to bullshit and stretch out my word count so I can say, "I wrote a book!" I'm not going to say one thing and write it out in a dozen different ways. Or a hundred different ways. Or a thousand different ways. This isn't middle school. Dammit! This is not middle school. And I'm not a cheat. A poor writer? Yes. A guy with no idea why anyone would be interested in reading 50,000 of my words? Absolutely. But a guy who will cheat or shortchange a reader? No way.

So what is this amateur "not long enough to be a book" about? Well, probably about 25,000 words. I'm just writing a bunch of short stories in response to questions I should have been asked. They aren't short stories because of the length of the answers. They're stories about being short, which, you probably already realize, has been a huge factor in my life.

My insecurities, drive to achieve, and humor are related to my height. To be clear, I'm not an LP, or little person. And the slights I've experienced can't be compared to the discrimination and challenges that little people endure daily. I'm not one of the "stop, stare, and point" little people. I'm more of a "sit in the front row and hold the second-grade class sign for the school photo" short, the "we're casting you as the family pet in the school play" short, or the "hold still, punk, while my girlfriend punches you in the face" short. This isn't all bad. I'm the perfect height for airline travel, especially coach.

Even then, there is a downside. On a plane with unassigned seats, by not taking up much space, the adjacent seat becomes very appealing to passengers walking up the aisle. Or down the aisle? Whatever. Folks coming towards you. It would be, at the very least, rude, and possibly unlawful to deny an adjacent seat to a fellow passenger. But there's nothing wrong with at times holding the barf bag to your chin to discourage some folks from sitting next to you.

Can anyone blame a five-foot, six-inch teenage boy for having insecurities? Last picked for sports as a kid and looked down on as a potential boyfriend by girls who grew up with images of looking up at their boyfriend. Heightism isn't my own weird perception. It's an empirically proven fact.

I'll never forget watching an investigative news show story on women wanting to date taller men. They had five women behind a two-way mirror with two equally attractive men on the other side. One man was five-foot-four and the other six-foot-two. The following discussion took place:

Moderator: Who would you rather date?
All women: The tall guy!
Moderator: Okay. Let me tell you some additional facts.
    The tall guy is a fry cook at Tony's Chicken Palace and
    Lube Barn, and the shorter guy is a medical doctor.
All women: The tall guy!

Moderator: Okay, just one more thing before you decide.
The shorter man loves children and enjoys gourmet
cooking. The taller guy has a felony record.
All women: (slight fraction-of-a-second pause) What kind
of felony?

What kind of felony? Are you kidding me? Is it any
wonder I have height insecurity? I have almost daily
reminders that I'm vertically challenged. I'm reminded
when I'm standing nose to armpit on a crowded elevator.
I'm reminded because in my new driver's license photo, you
can see my feet. Not a crippling insecurity, mind you. Not a
diagnosed mental illness.

Admittedly, I've never had a mental health evaluation.
Remember when our 45th president said that if we didn't
do so many COVID-19 tests, we'd have fewer cases of the
virus? I decided that if I never had a mental health
evaluation, I couldn't be mentally ill. Knowing myself as
long as I have, I'm guessing if I had any real serious mental
issues, I'd have spotted them. On the other hand, Jeffery
Dahmer probably said, "I'm fine. It's all those people I ate
who had mental health issues."

From an early age, I could quickly diagnose neuroses
and character flaws in others. I could talk to someone for
less than two minutes and quickly conclude, "Wow, that guy
is really insecure" or "He's a jerk." Two minutes of
conversation was really all it took. In fact, sometimes I
didn't even have to talk to someone to make my diagnosis.
On many occasions, I could just see someone across a room,
watch him raise an eyebrow and, without a word having
been spoken, conclude, "That guy looks like an arrogant
asshole."

Despite the lack of a professional assessment, I realized
that many insecurities, personality traits, and even
friendships throughout my life were influenced by my
height. It took me a while to realize how much my short
stature affected all aspects of my life. I decided to jot down

these short stories after emptying a storage shed full of old boxes I'd saved for decades. There were notebooks with entries I'd written about trying to fit in, giving in to peer pressure to try to be popular, and musings about women I wanted to date.

The storage shed with the boxes of notebooks had other treasures, valuable stuff like my 1974 animal psychology class notes, a toaster that only toasted one side of the bread I got as a wedding present in 1985, and a 1982 Iowa road map. The folks on Storage Wars would have been disappointed.

Why did I save this junk? Was I a hoarder or just too lazy to spend time going through them? Did I think someday I'd need to see how highways in Dubuque had changed over forty years? Did I think future historians would examine these papers in some college archive? "Gee, Elliot must have really been fascinated by Harlow's studies on rhesus monkeys." Did I think someone would want to know if I liked only one-sided toast?

I decided to rid myself of all this junk, which is easier said than done. It was way too much to put in a trash can, even if I spread it out over several months. My first thought was to give people the opportunity to steal my boxes by wrapping them in brown paper and leaving them in the back of my car. I decided against it because someone might get pissed at what they'd gotten and come back and mess up my car.

My solution to dispose of storage shed boxes: Goodwill. Thank God for Goodwill. They take anything. It feels good to get rid of all your junk and get a tax deduction for doing it, especially since Goodwill uses the honor system to put a cash value on your donation. How cool is that? You donate stuff, deduct it on your taxes, and you decide what your junk is worth! I'm heading there later today to give them my thousand-dollar toaster and one-hundred-dollar antique Iowa map. It feels good to donate, doesn't it? Whenever there's a food drive, I generously donate all the pumpkin pie filling and cans of sauerkraut that have cluttered my pantry.

But you're not reading this for financial planning or tax advice. No, you're reading this because I gave it to you as a gift, and you're just hoping this will end. And I appreciate that. Just like you appreciate that this rambling introduction/prologue/amateurlogue is finally over. I still hate Tom Jones, and I got over 1,500 words in this chapter.

CHAPTER 6

How Did Your Parents Choose Your Name?

My parents, like many Jews, had a tradition of naming their child after a deceased relative. (This is why so many young Jewish boys are named Grandpa.) My understanding is the tradition is based on the hope that the child will have the same fine qualities of the decedent and that he or she will want to learn about the family history. I'm named for my great-grandfather Isadore Zacks, who died in 1949. How does the name Elliot come from Isadore? It doesn't. But our Hebrew names are the same: Yisrael Esau. Thankfully, in my family, it was enough that the English name was similar to the English name of the deceased as long as the Hebrew name was the same. Fortunately, they didn't feel compelled to name me Isadore, which would have sucked. "Hey, Isadore bigger than a window?" Or maybe I'd be called Izzy. "Hey, Izzy anybody's friend?" I was never a fan of the name Elliot, but at least it's not Isadore. Growing up, and to this day, my oldest friends and family call me Lee.

Since I didn't need to be Isadore, why couldn't I have had a normal name like Mike or Joe? I was born on August 23. Was there a quota on normal names that had been reached in the days before my birth? Was Joe unavailable after July? If that was the case, I could certainly understand my mom not wanting to be pregnant for thirteen months until the following January, when presumably Joe again would be available. But why Elliot? Elliot sounds like a short, nerdy, sickly Jewish kid with a briefcase, which is very unfortunate since I was a short, sickly, nerdy Jewish kid. And my folks said a six-year-old with a briefcase looked adorable.

Feeling obliged through religion, tradition, ego, or otherwise to give your child a family name is a horrible reason to saddle your kid with a label that's going to follow them forever. Just because a name was popular a hundred years ago doesn't mean you should stick your kid with it. All of you with an affinity for passing along Harold, Arthur, Maurice, Chester, or Todd (with apologies to any Harolds, Arthurs, Maurices, Chesters, or Todds out there), stop it. Just stop! If you don't believe me, ask my friend Adolf.

Naming your child is your first important parenting decision. Kids are mean little assholes, and your selection of a name will impact your son or daughter's entire childhood and consequently their entire life. Trust me on this one. Name your kid Elliot, and it's "Elliot Smelliot." Name your daughter Jill, and it's "Jill the Pill." You don't want your kid coming up to you in twenty years saying, "Thanks Mom and Dad for the dick name." Go ahead. Name your kid Gary and watch him be a loser for life (with apologies to any Garys out there).

Yet there's an exception to the rule that a jerky name will ruin a kid's life. In recent years, celebrities, because they're rich and their kids all go to private school, have decided to show their superiority by giving their children the stupidest, most ridiculous name they can mash up. "Class, I want you all to meet our newest students, Garbage Truck Celery Stalk, her brother King Douchebag Moondust, and their bodyguards Zeus and Hercules." In regular schools, a guy gets beat up if he's named Willie. Consider naming your kid Killer. No one will ever mess with her, and it will give her character.

My daughter is Jill, and I had nothing to do with her

name selection. I didn't meet her until she was ten. I have no biological or legal relationship with her, but she is 100 percent my daughter as much as my sons, whose names I did help select. For what it's worth, I like the name Jill, even though it isn't very common. She wasn't a big fan of mine when I began dating her mom. Understandable since her dad was no longer around, and the guy Lorraine had been engaged to between her divorce and our marriage wasn't around either. Since I wasn't around when she was little, I don't know if insensitive, immature children cruelly taunted her as "Jill the Pill", but it was fun for me.

Deciding on a kid's name should be done in advance of their birth. Responsible couples will spend hours selecting a name. I say "responsible couples" because I'm guessing anyone who named their son Adam or Aaron consulted a baby name book at the last minute and wasn't motivated to read past the As. Unless you're Pinocchio, more time should be spent picking a name than picking your nose. When I tell you not to wait to select a name, I speak from experience. When our first child was born, we figured the kid would look like someone, and we'd come up with a name. For those of you without children, those of you with both sanity and some semblance of a life, let me clue you in. When a baby is born, they don't look like anyone. They all look like they've been in a terrible accident. The only name that came into my mind was Rex, spelled Wrecks. My kid came out all purple. He looked like a grape with hair. Had Lorraine cheated on me with Papa Smurf? To our great relief, Welches grew up a happy, well-adjusted child.

While Welches seemed fitting, there were no deceased Welches relatives or even a Wally. So we ditched the name Welches and went with Ben in honor of my late grandmother Bertha, a name we would never have chosen even if we'd had a daughter. I guess we could have named our son Bert, but that had too much of a Sesame Street vibe, and we'd have probably felt compelled to name a younger sibling Ernie.

Ben was adorably cute. Cherubic face. Dimples. Curly

light brown hair. Shortly after he was born, our pediatrician told us Ben had to wear orthopedic shoes because his feet pointed in. These shoes were designed to straighten his feet. They had a metal bar between them to hold his feet in place. Ben had to lie in bed with his feet in these shoes and the bar between them. He couldn't turn over. He just had to lie there. It killed me to see him like that. On the bright side, the metal bar made a nice handle. I could carry the little guy like a briefcase, a way cooler briefcase than I carried at age six. It not only made a nice carrier but I could hang him on a hook when I showered. That was cool. But other than that, the orthopedic shoes were unpleasant. At least Ben wore this contraption before he could walk. Hopping around in orthopedic shoes would have likely been difficult, and kids would likely have ridiculed that more than if we'd named him Gary.

Our second kid was Zach. His first name has nothing to do with any dead relative. But his two middle names, Jordan and O'Day, are for my uncle George Glicksman and Lorraine's grandfather Raymond O'Day. Zach was different from Ben. Zach was different from everyone. His first word was not "mama" or "dada." It was "no." He didn't have an imaginary friend. He had an imaginary enemy, Dobie. With Ben, we could just give him a disapproving look to express our disappointment, and he would cry and never repeat whatever transgression he had done. A scowl or crossways look would never deter Zach. At two years old, I spanked him, very gently, just to get his attention so that he'd stop misbehaving. He looked directly into my eyes and said, "That didn't hurt." That didn't hurt? He was stubborn and refused to surrender to parental authority, even over little things. If he didn't want to be put in his car seat, he'd arch his back and struggle to stay out.

Reasoning with Zach was a waste of time. When Zach turned four, he received and spent a $2.50 gift certificate from a local toy store. Three weeks later, his brother, Ben, turned six and received a similar gift certificate. At the toy store, Zach couldn't understand why Ben now got to buy a toy and he could not. When Lorraine explained that he had already bought his present on his birthday a few weeks earlier, Zach told his mom that he "hated" her. The following is a verbatim transcript of the discussion that ensued:

> Lorraine: (incredibly calmly) Zach, it really hurts my feelings when you tell me you hate me. It makes me want to cry.
>
> Zach: Then why aren't you crying?
>
> Lorraine: It really hurts my feelings when you say that to me. What would you do if I said that to you?
>
> Zach: I would call the police and have you arrested.
>
> Lorraine: Is that what you want me to do?
>
> Zach: Oh. I guess you just want the police to come and put handcuffs on me and take me away to jail. And then you wouldn't have a little boy who just turned four. Is that what you want?

As parents, every day revolved around our kids' activities, dance classes and recitals, basketball, volleyball, baseball, chess tournaments, school projects, and Hebrew school. Vacations focused solely on what they'd enjoy. With both of us working and trying to steal just a few minutes for ourselves, it was hectic and exhausting. There were many nights when Jill would have dance practice or the boys would have baseball practice at two different fields. Coaches or teachers would throw off our dinner or homework schedules when practices ran late. Life was crazy and exhausting, and looking back, I wonder how we did it. We couldn't wait for that period of our lives to be over. Today, I'd give almost anything to go back and spend ten minutes watching Jill dance or the boys play Little League.

Before ending this missive, it's important to point out that it's not just the names we give our children that are important. The names we assign everything create a filter for how things are viewed. If you call Medicare or Social Security an entitlement, it sounds bad. Why should anyone be entitled to free stuff from the government? On the other hand, if we refer to these programs as *earned benefits*, that certainly sounds like something we paid for and shouldn't have taken away.

How we name things influences how we view those things. Why would a hospital ever have "Memorial" in its name? Even leading facilities like Sloane Kettering Memorial. Really? If I'm in an ambulance and the driver says, "I'm taking you to Memorial," I'm not feeling real optimistic about my prognosis. "Hey, driver, save yourself some gas money and let me off at Forest Lawn." I got a better idea. "Hey, driver, how 'bout you take me to the Sloan Kettering Gets You Better So You Don't Die Hospital?"

Hospitals are really the worst at naming medical conditions. Patients are *critical*. Who wouldn't be? Ever eat hospital food? You bet he's critical. He hit the call button, waited for an hour, and then crapped the bed. For that he should be appreciative? You hear a doctor say someone's in grave condition. Really? Grave condition? That's a real glass-half-empty kind of hospital! Should we all grab shovels?

Okay, I guess I got a little off track here. I guess I could have just answered the question of how I got my name by saying it was in memory of a deceased relative. That's the answer to the question right there.

Ben, Zach, and Jill

Chapter 7

What Religion are You?

I'm not a member of any organized religion. I'm Jewish. My wife, Lorraine, is Catholic, which I really didn't appreciate until she gave me up for Lent. Being a Jew, I had no idea Lent lasted nine months. I've always loved being a Jew. I recently saw a piece on CNN that a public relations firm is using Superman, who was created by two Jews in the 1920s, as the basis for a Christian sermon. I was pissed. First you take Jesus from us and now Superman. As a people, we've had enough suffering. Please leave us Mel Brooks.

I don't like religion when it's used to make laws, kill people, or sell stuff, including dating services. Christian Mingle is an internet dating site promising to find God's match for you. If God wanted to find you a match, would he really need an internet dating site to do it? According to the folks who make money from this website, before the internet, God didn't give a shit if Christians got a booty call.

I enjoy the religious rituals and pageants. Every person should attend a Passover Seder. No matter what your religion, or lack of religion, a Passover Seder is the meal to begin a celebration of freedom. Every holiday in every culture has its special holiday food. Thanksgiving has your turkey and pumpkin pie. Easter has its ham and Easter eggs. The Passover delicacies are the matzo and the gefilte fish. Yeah, that's messed up. Gefilte fish is unlike any fish a gentile has ever seen. It's a round fish. A round ball of fish, to be precise. The gefilte must be endangered because you won't find one in a restaurant. You'll never hear a waiter say, "Good evening, I'm Claude. I'll be assisting you tonight. For this evening's special, the chef is preparing a lovely broiled gefilte. It will be finished with horseradish to mask the taste." The endangered gefilte also can't be found at a supermarket fresh fish counter.

Understandably, measures are being taken right now to preserve the endangered gefilte. In fact, it's preserved in a glass jar. If you've never seen gefilte fish, it resembles a white fishy sort of meatball suspended in a sea of what looks like Vaseline. Yes, the gefilte is to fish what McNuggets are to chicken.

The other Passover delicacy is matzo, which can be used to make matzo balls. Matzo balls are white round ... well, they look a lot like gefilte fish without being surrounded by a petroleum-based solution. Matzo balls are white-meatball-type things. Of course, matzo in its native form is a giant flavorless cracker. A big flat cracker the size of an iPad. And it's a Passover food because it was created when the Jews were released from bondage. I heard it's important to have a safe word for that. But back when Jews built the pyramids, the Pharaoh was reluctant to free them. When he finally freed them, the Jews were in such a hurry that they didn't have time to let their bread rise, so ... matzo.

During the eight-day Passover celebration, matzo is substituted for bread, which wouldn't be bad if the matzo didn't fall apart after the first bite. You grab the matzo, and after one bite, you're left holding two small pieces of matzo between the thumb and forefinger of each hand while the rest of the matzo sits on your lap. That's why peanut butter is a good matzo spread. It holds the matzo together.

When I was a kid, our sandwich meat was often tongue. Remember when you first realized that the chicken you were eating was really a chicken or that the burger you were eating was really a cow? I had that revelation when I was eating tongue during Passover. When I was nine years old, my mom packed my school lunch with a slice of tongue between two pieces of matzo. During the lunch period, I already felt goofy pulling the mortar-board-sized saltine from my lunch bag. As I bit into this communion wafer on steroids, I wound up with those little pieces of matzo between the thumb and forefinger of each hand like unleavened castanets. Giant cracker slabs rained down my shirt and into my lap. But the tongue—this thick, long, eight-inch slice of tongue—hung from my mouth and down my neck like a nine-year-old Gene Simmons.

Before we got married, Lorraine agreed to raise our children in the Jewish faith. Lorraine and her daughter, Jill, remained Catholic. Christmas and Chanukah confused our Jewish sons. They walked around the house singing "Oy Vey Maria" and "Deck the Halls with Matzo Balls." Utterly clueless.

Chanukah is a very minor religious celebration except for its proximity to Christmas. Like Passover, Chanukah lasts eight nights. A child is to receive a present each and every night of Chanukah. That was and is the custom, the tradition. My parents did not have a lot of money, but they understood and maintained that tradition. You can imagine my anticipation in 1964, at the age of 10, opening my first-night present. I still remember ripping off the blue and white wrapping paper, and there inside was GI Joe. Well, not actually GI Joe. I got GI Joe's head. His head! At that point, even at the age of 10, I figured out what the next seven nights were going to bring. Ironically, at this point in my life, I wouldn't mind a little head on the first night of Chanukah.

I had the opportunity to compare Catholicism and Judaism, and frankly the Catholics made some good updates when they branched off a couple thousand years ago. The collection plate, for example. How the hell did we miss that one? Their method of repentance was a big improvement as well. Lent is an obvious upgrade over Yom Kippur.

For Lent, Catholics give up something they supposedly like for 40 days. It can be chocolate or alcohol or kelp, just something. Jews, on the other hand, renounce everything they need to live except air for 24 hours. From sunset to sunset, for one day, Jews give up all food and drink, even water, while we go and pray (quite a bit of it while standing).

While practicing law, I once explained to Judge Mike Brown that I wouldn't be able to attend a hearing the following week because it fell on Yom Kippur. From the bench, I remember his booming voice saying, "Oh, yeah, sure, everyone's Jewish on Yom Kippur."

"No," I responded, "everyone's Irish on Saint Patty's Day. No one wants to be Jewish on Yom Kippur, not even the Jews."

I'm not religious. I don't attend services except maybe a day or two each year. Nevertheless, it was important to raise my children Jewish. If countless efforts to eradicate my religion from pogroms, the Inquisition, and Hitler had failed, I sure as hell wasn't going to contribute to its elimination. I would not be responsible for a world without kreplach, rugelach, and other delicacies that are pronounced correctly only while clearing your throat.

Lorraine agreed that while she'd remain Catholic, we would raise our kids Jewish. Of course, had she known about a bris, the party folks attend with food and drink eight days after a Jewish boy's birth to celebrate whacking off the tip of his dick, I have no doubt she'd have required that we raise the world's only uncircumcised Jew.

My sons, Ben and Zach, attended Hebrew school—"Jew school," as they called it—and had their bar mitzvah. As far as I was concerned, at that point I had completed whatever obligation I felt to the millions who had preceded me, many of whom had been evicted from their homes, tortured, and killed to preserve their right to worship as they wanted.

My relief at not having contributed to my faith's attrition was short lived when Lorraine suggested that our sons attend a nearby Catholic high school. Parochial schools of any faith repulsed me as homogeneous groups of spoiled children. But our neighborhood high school had more violence than a *Soprano*'s episode. Our choice was to either move to a new school district or send our Jewish sons to Salpointe Catholic.

Salpointe was run by the Carmelites, which, to this Jew, sounded like a 60s girl group fronted by Darlene Love. Or a diet candy, like Ayds, the unfortunately named appetite-suppressing candy of the early 1980s that helped you lose weight. Nightly news stories of emaciated, dying AIDS patients during that same period of time led to the diet supplement's demise.

Any question I had about whether Jewish kids could attend a Catholic school were quickly answered. Salpointe accepted all denominations: tens, twenties, fifties, and also credit cards.

I had concerns that my sons would be teased or picked on for being Jews or pressured to convert to Catholicism so they wouldn't burn in hell for eternity. None of my concerns was well founded. My sons were picked on because they were short, uncoordinated and so on, but not for being Jews. And becoming a Catholic like their mom had zero appeal. Although they attended Mass weekly and had a photograph of the pope in every classroom, they seemed oblivious to the religion all around them. When I asked my son Zach what he thought of having the pope's picture in his class, he told me he thought it was the principal. This explained the headmaster's confusion when my son would pass him in the hallway and say, "Hey, where's your hat?"

The senior class at Salpointe had series of three-day, two-night retreats led by some of the fathers and brothers of the order as well as students who had previously gone on a retreat and had been selected to be leaders of future retreats. These were profound experiences for students, who were not allowed their phones or watches. Over the course of the days, students opened up about their most personal life experiences. Sexuality, addictions, and abuse in these teenagers' lives were shared. It was a serious, sacred experience. Except for Zach, who convinced a group of boys to streak naked through the campground on the final day of the retreat.

After convincing the school and parents that he

shouldn't be criminally prosecuted for indecent exposure, contributing to the delinquency of minors, and a host of other crimes, Zach was surprised and dismayed to learn he wouldn't be selected as a leader on future retreats. I was disappointed for him, but I really thought he'd have seen it coming when he was required to send letters of apology to every student who attended and their parents or when he had to clean the campground after the next few retreats.

While I am not religious, I enjoy many religious traditions, including the traditions of decorating homes with Christmas lights. In Tucson, there's a neighborhood called Winterhaven, where residents compete for prizes based on their decor. Winterhaven prohibits all nonresident motor vehicles during the weeknights before Christmas so that families, horse-drawn carriages, and bicyclists can enjoy the festivities. Carolers sing songs, and occasionally a performer will do a Christmas-themed reading. It's a very family-oriented event, except one time in 2019, when a very stoned, opportunistic panhandler with a steel drum tried to solicit funds from the crowd with his novel interpretation of "The Little Drummer Boy."

"Hey, everybody. Bob Girth here, and I'd like to perform one of the most beloved Christmas stories. I'm pretty sure it's in the Bible—not the Old Testament, the Bible 2.0. So please enjoy my reenactment of 'The Little Steel Drummer Boy.' I have no gifts to bring. The only gift I have to give the baby Jesus is the gift of my music emanating from these steel drums." (At this junction, the guy began banging his drum like Gene Krupa doing "Sing Sing Sing.")

"It's the only gift I have to give the baby Jesus. There I am playing, and what does Mother Mary say? She says, 'What's with the drums? Enough with the drums already! Can't you see I got a baby here trying to sleep?' But I can't really hear her 'cause I'm parumpumping the heck out of my drum. Then I hear Joseph say, 'What's all that racket? God isn't visiting you again, is he?' And Mary goes, 'No, it's some guy banging on pots and pans.' But I still can't hear her. So I'm parumpumping, and suddenly baby Jesus wakes up, and he's screaming like a banshee. So baby Jesus is screaming, and Mary and Joseph go ballistic, yellin' at me. And they start throwing stuff at me, not at the tip jar— which, by the way, is right here for any of you Winterhaven visitors. No, they're throwing frankincense at me. No gold, that's for darn sure. No silver either. And Mary goes, 'Hey, how 'bout you stop the parumpumping and at least play some Christmas music for Chrissakes.' And I say, 'Who do I look like, Bing Crosby?' But there are two songs I can play. One is 'No Woman No Cry,' and the other isn't. So I play 'No Woman No Cry,' and sure enough the baby Jesus stops crying. I look at Mary, and she smiled at me. Me and my drum. Just like it says in the Bible."

While I found Girth's performance amusing, many festival attendees did not. In the true spirit of Christmas, my last image that evening was Bob Girth getting beaten by a Winterhaven resident dressed as an elf with a staff he'd removed from his front yard manger diorama.

CHAPTER 8

What Differences Have You Observed between Men and Women?

As a retiree, I observe things that busy people may not appreciate, like the fact that men are different from women. Not in the obvious ways like the fact that a woman will get out of a shower to pee, or a bathtub, or a truck. The biggest difference between men and women is that women don't brag about themselves. My wife can spend a 12-hour day cleaning our house, vacuuming, paying bills, doing laundry, doing volunteer work, shopping, and cooking and not say a word about it. Nothing. I get up in the morning and take out one bag of garbage. I come back in the house, look at my wife and say, "See any garbage? Probably not ... because it's gone. I took it out. Gone!" And when I empty the dishwasher, I want a parade. I'm kidding. I never empty the dishwasher. I have no idea where any of that stuff goes.

Guys brag. I spent five, maybe ten minutes putting in a dimmer switch. For the next six months, anyone who came to my house heard about it. Even if they were within range of my house, they heard about it: "Hey, Joe, come on in here. Wanna see something cool? I wanna show you something. Leave your dog outside ... no, leave him outside. Okay, bring him in. Check this out. Go ahead, turn it. Bright ... dim. Bright ... dim. Hey, is that the UPS guy out there?" Fine. You caught me. I'm kidding about this. I have no idea how to install a dimmer switch.

You're probably wondering whether I'm handy around the house. You might ask, "Hey, Elliot, are you handy around the house?" I'd say, "No. No, I'm not handy." I can't fix things or repair things or maintain things. Even little things. If a light bulb goes out, I'll ask Lorraine, "Do we need so much light? Why do we need this much light?" If two or three more lights burn out, I'll ask Lorraine, "Do we need this house? Why do we need this house? Plus it's kind of dark in here."

Not being handy is in my DNA. For the most part, Jewish men can't fix or build things. It's so rare that the last time we had a Jewish carpenter, they based a religion on it. Jews are doctors and lawyers. And the Jewish lawyers are just the Jews who can't stand the sight of blood. Building isn't in our DNA. After we built the pyramids, there was a collective "That's it! Enough with the building already." As I've documented, my wife, who can fix stuff and not brag about it, was raised Catholic.

The extent to which women don't brag about themselves, however, is inversely proportional to the extent to which they will brag about their children. A mom will tell you how great their son was in Little League and proudly display his participation ribbon. She'll tell you how her daughter was potty trained at the age of two as you watch her kid stumble around the room, crapping in some sort of diaper/underpants thing. In fairness, it's pretty hard to explain to a toddler why they have to go into a bathroom when they've spent their entire life crawling around with a toilet wrapped around their butt.

Women will brag about their child's most inconsequential achievement. Before I had kids of my own, a time of my life I call "the joyous period of disposable income," my neighbor Elizabeth insisted I come over because her 18-

month-old could say the entire Pledge of Allegiance. So off I go to hear young Einstein recite the pledge. Granted, the kid was able to say the Pledge of Allegiance. But it wasn't like he had it memorized. He had to read it! Took him, like, five minutes to sound out *indivisible*.

I don't recall having a lot of toys as a kid. I think Rodney Dangerfield said, "If I weren't a boy, I wouldn't have had anything to play with." I certainly had toys, but I don't remember many of them. Of course, there's a lot I don't remember. At least I think there's a lot I don't remember. If I knew for sure, I'd remember. In any event, the toys I had were just a gateway to using my imagination.

The first toy I recall was a rocking horse connected on each of its four corners by springs. As a small boy, I remember rocking for long periods of time. I should probably say "young boy" since I was a small boy until I became a small man. As a young boy from the ages of four to maybe seven, I can remember being in my bed on all fours and rocking back and forth to fall asleep. My folks tell me I even did this as a baby in my crib. My baby head would butt against the wall of the crib, and with each strike the crib would move an inch or two. One time, it moved so far that I blocked the bedroom door, actually barricading it to prevent my parents' entry. That early beating of my head against the crib likely explains why I don't remember much about my toys. That or the marijuana I smoked as a teenager.

Whatever the reason, I don't have many vivid memories of toys. What I do remember is that without the internet or Xbox, I created my own stories. I had little plastic army men to play army. I had cowboy hats and guns to play cowboy. Like I said, toys were just a tool for my imagination.

The Man from UNCLE was a television series that ran between 1964 and 1968, when I was ten to fourteen years old. It was a spy series that arose from the success of the James Bond movies. UNCLE stood for the United Network Command for Law Enforcement. Okay, I can remember some stuff but mostly only useless stuff from television.

When households had only one phone, back when you had no idea who was calling until you picked up, the phone company made a push for people to buy more phones. They called it an extension phone. The jingle included the lines:

Just reach for an extension,
And we might mention
You go right on doing things.
Sure is the handiest time-saver known,
The handy little invention
The extension phone.

It seemed crazy to have a second phone when often you couldn't use the one you had. In the early 1960s, when you picked up a phone, you sometimes stepped into the middle of another conversation. Or someone else would pick up a phone and listen to yours. It was called a party line. You didn't know the people with whom you were sharing a phone line, and people who were talking got pissed if you stayed on longer than they thought necessary for you to realize someone else was using the phone.

From there, we went to a culture where there was a phone in every room, so when we were at home we wouldn't be too far when someone called. Now we take our phones with us. Cell phones weren't around until I was in my 50s, and the first time someone offered their cell number, I thought they were calling me from jail.

Cell phones now allow anyone to reach us anytime. You're never away from work. Until the recent past, once you left your work you were, for the most part, unreachable. Today, you're never unreachable. People call, text, and email you on your phone, and if you don't respond to a text or an email within minutes, you get another text or email asking why you're so rude.

People bring their phones everywhere. Last week, I stood next to a guy at a urinal on his phone discussing a business deal. On the one hand, I figured it must have been really important if it couldn't wait until he left the bathroom. On the other hand, I wondered how important a business deal could be when the guy at the other end of the call was being serenaded by flushing toilets. Why would someone urinating in a public restroom want to have a serious phone call? Maybe he was just holding up the phone and pretending to talk the way I do when I'm walking down the street and see someone I don't want to talk to. Maybe there was no business deal at all, and he just pretended to talk about one to impress me. Hey, you want to impress me? Wash your hands before you grab the doorknob, which, by the way, is hard to do when you're holding your phone. That and one-handed zipping up.

We're all addicted to our phones. If we misplace our phones, a panic previously reserved for losing your child in a department store sets in. I'm certainly guilty of spending way too much time on my phone. And you know you're spending too much time on your phone when Apple sends you a text telling you that your iPhone use is up 28 percent from the previous month. You have a bad phone jones when the product tells you to get a hobby. This is a serious intervention. After eating a Big Mac, McDonalds doesn't text a suggestion to try a plant based diet.

I don't have email on my phone because I'd have a Pavlovian response every time I heard a ding. And I usually don't answer my phone if I don't recognize the number because when I do, it's someone telling me I won a cruise, that my car warranty is about to expire, or asking me if I need a new windshield.

And you can't block these solicitations. They have a whole phone bank of people making cold calls to sell you stuff, so if you block one number, the next guy calls you tomorrow. It has to be tough doing phone solicitations and having nearly everybody hanging up on you. My guess is that most of the telemarketers are Jehovah's Witnesses who spent years having doors slammed in their faces, so, by comparison, someone hanging up on them is no big deal.

What was I writing about? It wasn't phones, was it? No. Definitely not phones. Oh, yeah. Toys. My favorite toys. The man from UNCLE had a gun in a shoulder holster. So I had a toy gun in a shoulder holster. James Bond had a briefcase that had all sorts of gadgets in it. So I had a briefcase with all sorts of gadgets in it. TV was a huge influence. One show I absolutely loved was the *Wild Wild West,* another spy show set in the mid-1800s. Jim West, played by Robert Conrad, always wore three-piece suits and looked cool as hell in his vest. When I was bar mitzvahed in 1967, I insisted on having a three-piece suit. And I wore one. I thought I looked cool as hell in my vest. At least, that's what I remember. But remember, I really can't remember shit.

Postscript to Jewish readers: Yes, I know bar mitzvahed is not a word. The correct phrase is became a bar mitzvah. I know.

Postscript to non-Jewish readers who want to sound Jewish: Here's a tip. Use the word "from" instead of "about" to sound Jewish. For example, instead of saying "He doesn't know about basketball," try "He doesn't know from basketball." See what I mean? By the way, there haven't been many Jewish basketball players. With a name like that, I assume Julius Erving was one, especially since he was a doctor.

CHAPTER 9

What Were Your Most Humiliating Life Experiences?

Finally. I wondered when you'd ask about sex. Certainly, my most humiliating experiences have all been sex. And this goes back to my youth. In my teens, there were days I'd think about sex hundreds of times. And there were other days I really thought about sex a lot. I felt tremendous pressure to get laid. Everyone was doing it! I was a teenager entering my prime, living in the sweet spot, the era after the pill and before incurable sexually transmitted diseases. I was a single guy alive during the golden era of free love, and no-consequence sex. No one had to worry about getting pregnant or getting AIDS. Every *Playboy* I read suggested that for everyone but me, life was one big hedonistic orgy. Even Henry Kissinger was getting laid. But not me.

Over time, I wondered if I'd ever have sex. And if there was someone out there willing to have sex with me, would I want to be with someone that had such low standards?

I worried whether I would be a good lover. I practiced constantly in my free time. It's been written that you need to do something ten thousand times to become an expert. Ten thousand times doing the same thing and you're an expert? If that's true, in the time I wasted "practicing" during high school and college, I could have become fluent in Spanish, completed a paint-by-numbers scale version of the Sistine Chapel, and learned to play the flute.

How would I even know if I was a good lover? Everyone thinks they're good lovers, just like they think they're good drivers. And most people drive like Yoko Ono sings. Despite being the Shakespeare of shaking it, the Mickey Mantle of milking it, knowing the Magic of my Johnson and the Wonka of my Willie, I worried I'd be a shitty lover. Worries that I later learned were well founded.

I lost my virginity in college and never looked for it again. I was fortunate to have attended college in the 1970s, after the invention of the birth control pill. So significant was this development that despite millions of pills on the market for countless medical conditions, only one was known as "the pill." Women no longer feared an unwanted pregnancy. And everyone had sex with everyone. All the time. Even me. And I could talk. Boy, could I talk. Maybe I was clever or funny. Maybe my short stature made me safe, or cute, or whatever. Maybe they were performing acts of charity. I didn't care why. I was thrilled they were willing to touch me. And I didn't have to beg. Well, maybe I didn't have to. I don't know. I still did.

Even after marriage, I continued to doubt my sexual prowess. I remember one magical night when Lorraine and I were in the middle of making love. I call it "the middle." I was finished. She was just barely starting. I averaged it. What I lacked in talent, technique, and prowess, I made up for with speed. I'm not so bad in bed as I am boring. Really sexually boring. When I masturbate, my hand falls asleep.

After 37 years of marriage, I've never cheated on my wife. Here I am married to Lorraine, a beautiful, kind woman. The very idea of being with other women in bed and disappointing them as well is just too much to deal with. I guess the silver lining to being a terrible lover is that the idea of having sex with anyone other than your spouse is humiliating and awful, and I'm not into that sort of thing. But I know there are some guys that'll pay extra for that.

No one should cheat on their spouse. Cheating is cheating, and you'll feel crappy if you do it. Whether you pay someone to take your kid's SAT exam, fake a photo of them on a water polo team, or cheat on your diet, it's all cheating, and you're going to regret it. Cheating on your wife can be like cheating on your diet. You've committed to a diet to lose weight. Made a vow to stay healthy. When you sit down for a meal and you tell yourself, "I'm not eating dessert. No way. I'm on a diet. Not gonna eat dessert" and then a piece of cake is offered to you, you didn't go looking for the cake. You didn't say, "Hey, I'm going out to look for some cake tonight." It's just there. Presented to you. Not an old cake that's been out for a while but a fresh, moist cake. And what happens if you eat the cake? I'll tell you what happens. As soon as you finish, the very second you finish, you say, "Why did I eat the cake?" You're racked with guilt. Just say no. Your craving for cake will pass. Maybe this wasn't the best analogy. Writing this made me really hungry. Wiping the crumbs off my lap, I'm thinking maybe cheating on your diet isn't as bad as cheating on your wife.

After 37 years of marriage, I've learned a lot. For example, I know ways to piss off my wife that I never imagined in my youth. And I finally know what she likes in bed. Sleep! Of course, I'm kidding. I have no idea what she likes in bed.

I don't even know what she likes in a bed. We went out to buy a new mattress. There are many mattress choices today: king, queen, Sleep Number, Craftmatic, and Posturepedic. When the salesman asked Lorraine what kind of bed she was interested in, she said, "Bunk." Because of all the different mattress options, there has been a proliferation of mattress stores. Three out of every four commercial corners has a mattress store. This may have some sort of correlation with the increase in the number of pillows per bed.

Lorraine and I got our new bed, and one night, things seemed to be going pretty well. We were going at it, and she started making these little moaning noises, sort of like the ones she makes at a Tom Jones concert but not exactly. I thought this was passion. It wasn't passion. Turned out I was lying across her arm. Her hand fell asleep. Which sucks because when that happens, everyone knows your hand is going to be up all night. In any event, at the time, I mistook her moaning for passion. When Lorraine stood up and began waving her right arm up and down, I had no idea what to do, so I started waving my right arm too. We looked like a couple of gamblers whose slot machines had vanished while we were playing.

Lorraine once suggested we see a sex therapist. I didn't want to see a sex therapist. I have read sex advice columns. The folks writing in to them have serious issues. One woman wrote, "My husband is constantly trying to have sex with me. I get up in the morning, he wants sex. I get home from work, he wants sex. After dinner, he wants sex. Please help me. I am at my wits' end. Sincerely, Desperate." Then at the bottom, it read, "PS: Please excuse the jerky handwriting." There was no way I was one of those losers who was going to a sex therapist.

The waiting room at the therapist's office was tastefully done. The Kinks' "You Really Got Me Going," in a format that could be used during a massage or meditation group, was playing. I told the counselor I was there for a friend. Millennial Dr. Ruth told Lorraine and me to try something crazy and erotic. She suggested an adult movie. This was in the early 1990s, before the internet or HBO. So we went to an adult movie house. I thought it was stupid. I was bored. Bored stiff. I don't remember what the movie was, but it had some clever 1990s name like *Rambone* or *Driving Miss Daisy Real Hard.*

But then I got into it. Even better, I could tell Lorraine was getting into it. It was cool except for this one guy. This guy was sitting next to me, of course, and throughout the movie, he was chokin' the chicken. I tried to ignore him. I really tried to ignore him, but he was using my hand.

Thanks to technology, I no longer need to go to a seedy theater to watch porn. I can just check out my kids' internet-browsing history.

In any event, despite a lifetime of copulation confusion and floundering fornication, Lorraine has hung with me since we began living together in 1984.

Me and the missus: Lorraine and me in the summer of 2021

CHAPTER 10

What Are Some of the Most Important Things You've Learned?

Here's a list of things I've learned:

1. If you want your favorite T-shirt to last a long time, never wear it.

2. Other than a car, if you give your spouse something that has a warranty, it's not a present. A toaster oven or vacuum cleaner is not a gift.

3. If you're at a party and awkwardly standing with two people, neither of whom know the other, introduce them to one another and tell each one something flattering about the other. It makes things much more comfortable for them. And it makes it easier for you to get away from them at the crummy party.

4. Sometimes when I pee, it sounds a little like banjo music.

5. Unless you're buying farm equipment or maybe tires, don't shop anywhere with "Barn" in its name, like Computer Barn or Electronics Barn or Dress Barn. (Sorry, even Pottery Barn, which doesn't sell pottery.)

6. Be a good tipper. The extra few bucks probably means nothing to you, and if it does, you ought to eat at home. While insignificant to you, a good tip can mean a lot to your server. Always over-tip them. Never tip them over.

51

7. If you're sitting at a restaurant for a long time to watch a baseball game, unless you're ordering a whole new meal each inning, generously tip the server when you arrive. Explain you'll be there for a few hours and tip them upfront so they aren't pissed off that they can't turn over your table. It's appreciated for many reasons, including the fact that each time a table is turned over, servers have to crawl around the floor to pick up the salt and pepper shakers.

8. Rock concert band etiquette: When you've finished your second-to-last song, don't leave the stage and keep the auditorium dark so you can hear us clapping and stomping our feet before you come back and do your last song, which you call an encore. How insecure are you? What more do we need to do to prove we like you? We already bought tickets. We're wearing your T-shirts and buying your ridiculously priced merch. Do you really need us to scream for five minutes for the encore number that's already printed on your setlist? Can't you just say, "This is our second-to-last song. We're not going to leave the stage and make you beg for us to come back. So consider this song to be our last song, but it'll really be the second-to-last song, so when it's done, we'll just stay here and do our encore."

9. Rock concert band etiquette: I love drum solos as much as the next guy, which is not very much. But there are few things more disheartening than watching a drum solo begin and seeing all the other band members leave the stage. "Wait a minute. Where are you all going?" If I have to sit here for this cacophony, you don't get to leave either. If you're not going to stay on the stage and listen, I'm hitting the beer line.

10. Rock concert fan etiquette: Unless the band asks the crowd to join in or points the microphone at the crowd, shut up. We get it. You're a fan. You know all the words to all their songs. Don't sing. Really.

11. If you're embarrassed about some personal trait or physical characteristic, make a joke about it. Folks like it when you make a self-deprecating joke. No asshole wants to tease someone about something that doesn't bother them.

Plus you'll hardly be sensitive at all about the ugly mole on your nose with a hair growing out of it that we're all staring at.

12. Teach your children to always give in to peer pressure. It's how they'll be popular.

13. When a dad takes his kid out and someone says, "Oh, babysitting today?" it is easy to be offended. You're a dad. You don't babysit your own kid. You spend time with them. Don't be offended. Don't argue that you're a father, not a babysitter, and that spending time with your child is what you do. Instead, look them in the eye, scratch your balls, and say, "Yeah, it's great. Ten bucks an hour and all the booze I can steal."

14. Have all of your bad habits before you get married. If you're about to get married and think someday you might want to smoke cigars or play poker or take a trip to Vegas every year with your buddies, start doing it before you get married so you can say, "Hey, you knew I did this when you married me." If you wait until after you're married to start any of these habits, you'll hear "So what's with the poker (Vegas, cigars, etc.)?"

15. It won't always be this way.

16. When you first listen to Cat Stevens's song "Father and Son," you're either the father or the son. Since the first time I heard it to this day, I'm always the son.

17. Bad times make good stories. Good times make boring stories.

18. If you fly with the owls at night, you gotta run with the hounds in the morning. I wasn't going to include this one, but since I drummed this into my kids when they were in high school and college (especially Zach), I needed to use it.

19. Never wear flip-flops at the Bayside bar urinal.

20. One should never turn on a light if changing the bulb would require climbing a ladder.

21. Unless the kid has a beard or is smoking a cigarette, never pass a lemonade stand without making a purchase. Pay twice what they are charging.

22. Support, encourage and build up everyone you meet. You never know what off-handed remark will be

meaningful or exactly what that person needed to hear.

23. If someone shows you something they made or bought that they are proud of or happy about, tell them how much you love it.

24. The older you get, the more work it takes to have fun.

In 2020, no one had fun. I have had requests about sharing my thoughts on the pandemic, but I'll write them anyway. The number 2020 used to refer to how many years had passed since Jesus was born. Or 2020 meant perfect vision. Not anymore. Now 2020 is synonymous with misery, an earthquake on top of a hurricane spinning off a rat infested tornado with color commentary by Joe Buck. People diagnosed with cancer say, "At least 2020 is over."

Still, 2020 grows in our collective memories like World War II and the Depression did with our parents. Fun? Fun? In 2020, going out and having fun changed from seeing the Rolling Stones in concert to shopping at Costco during senior hour. And if you found toilet paper, you'd post a picture on social media for the Facebook friends you've never met to like while you secretly hoped they'd be jealous of the cool life you had. Today's teenagers will tell their grandkids, "When I was your age, I had to use an old sock for my mask. It had holes in it and smelled like my grandmother" or "Virtual reality glasses? In 2020, we were lucky to have Netflix!"

Lorraine and me with the staff of the Bayside Tavern in Fish Creek, Wisconsin, 2018

CHAPTER 11

Can You Explain Aging?

Aging is like climbing up a mountain. The higher you go, the better the view. Hopefully, you don't forget the journey that got you there. That's not an original thought, but with humanity's ever-growing history, it's hard to ever have an original thought, isn't it? Recently, my local newspaper reported the death of a 65-year-old man who had been struck by a car while crossing the street. This bothered me. Not because a 65-year-old man was killed. Well, sure, that too. I was bothered by the description of a 65-year-old as "elderly." Did the writer know the man and describe him as elderly because he was a frail, stooped, aged fellow? Or was *elderly* used because, at 65, the man had crossed some threshold, and all 65-year-olds are elderly? Was this a media policy, or does the age at which one becomes elderly vary from writer to writer? Was this story written by an intern or a senior reporter? *Senior* meaning someone who has been a reporter for a long time, not someone just about to graduate high school.

I like getting older so much that I usually begin using my next age a few months before my birthday. Next August, I'll be 69, so around April, I'll start saying, "I'm about 69," which is weird, especially when no one asks how old I am. It's sort of like trying something on for a few months before you wear it. As of December 31, 2022, I had been alive for 24, 967 days. If you have your health, getting

55

older is a blessing. I'm lucky to find myself in the sweet spot of having free time, good health, adequate resources, and someone with whom to share my life. So at this point, I'm good with aging. But as I've written before, it won't always be this way.

I would just like aging to be more fun. For example, I need fiber for my colon, and I eat bran cereal till I'm shitting trees. But can't we make things like that more fun? Would it kill Kellogg to put a prize in the box? How cool would it be to fumble around wrist-deep in Raisin Bran and pull out a pair of reading glasses or, better yet, an inflatable lumbar support?

Longevity runs in my family. My 90-year-old mom has kept my baby book. She keeps it current. She's on volume 74: "Baby's First Colonoscopy. No polyps." Then she wrote, "Good job!" Gee, thanks, Mom. I'm sure it was the fiber.

Another feature of aging is my receding hairline. Really receding. "I could probably rent ad space on my forehead" receding. One advantage to a receding hairline is that my head looks longer and skinnier and people think I've lost weight. I'm actually trying to get in shape. During a recent consultation with a personal trainer, I was told I'd be considered fit if I could bench press my weight. When I get down to 47 pounds, I'll be a dynamo.

One of the concerns I have about aging is becoming invisible or irrelevant. Several years ago, Zach told me that I was invisible to younger women. "Fine," I replied. "They won't see me staring." I don't think I'm invisible to all young women. There's a woman at the neighborhood grocery store who always checks me out. I love it when she asks, "Paper or plastic?" I don't look forward to the day when a younger person tells my children, "Your dad is so together" simply because I can string together a sentence or don't yet drool into a bucket.

I have my own biases about young people. I understand that having a young doctor can be great because they keep current on the latest research and medical developments.

But I'm still weirded out when someone who looks like a kid is my doctor. When my doctor, who was my peer, retired, I was assigned to a new primary care physician. When she came in, I wondered if she was really a doctor or trying for her medical merit badge. I didn't know if she wanted to examine me or sell me cookies. When I asked how many years she'd been practicing, she held up three fingers and said, "This many." And she didn't believe any of my concerns. I swear she thought I was a hypochondriac. I get that. Lorraine thinks I exaggerate my symptoms. My sons think I'm a hypochondriac. Even my gynecologist says so. Finally, I convinced this doctor that I really was allergic to cotton. She prescribed some pills for it, but I can't get them out of the bottle. All of the jokes after the Girl Scout stuff are really old jokes. Told you it was hard to have an original thought.

I try to live a healthy lifestyle. In my youth, I exercised to get bigger and stronger. In middle age, I exercised to try to maintain the level of fitness I'd attained. My only goal now is to slow the deterioration. If I walk past someone in a gym, and they say, "What an ass," I know they're not referring to my physique. I don't judge anyone for getting cosmetic surgery. If it helps you feel confident in your appearance, fine. It's just not for me, although I have considered that surgery where they suck the fat out of you. It's called liposuction. I'm not sure if it's pronounced *lip-o-suction* or *lipe-o-suction*. I pronounce it *lip-o-suction* because it sounds more like something I'd enjoy. Doctors performing this procedure get paid to suck the fat out of you. For an additional price, they can shoot your fat back into you. They can suck fat from your thigh and shoot it into your forehead. They suck fat out of your butt and shoot it into your lips. You could literally kiss my ass.

I've developed a lot of old man habits. I wear sweater vests. I read the newspaper. Like many Arizonans, I dread reading the weather report between June and October. Tucson is dry and hot and getting drier and hotter. Outside

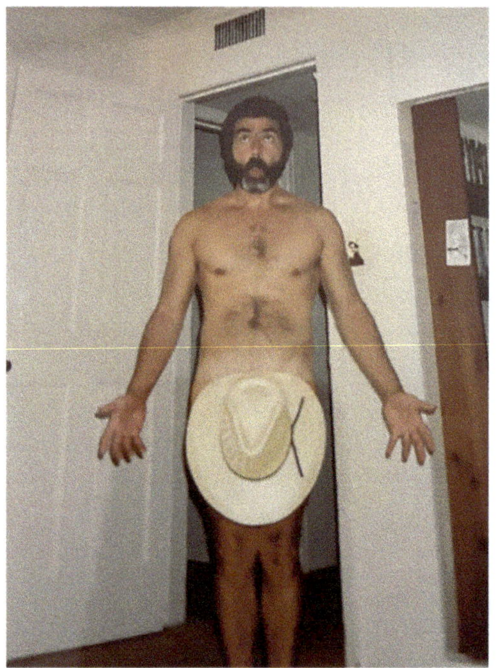

I sent out a cutout of this photo for my 40th birthday party with the caption "I can still get up for a big one ... yep for a big party."

of Arizona, you insult someone if you throw shade at them. Someone throws shade at me, I'm thrilled. Tucsonans will park a half mile from a store for a shady parking space, even if the shade is a one inch in diameter sapling.

My memories are comprised of many small moments and a few big ones. I wonder if some of my earliest memories are truly my memories or ones created from photos, old home movies, or stories I've heard. I know a woman who swears she remembers her father talking to her in the womb. Call me a skeptic, but even if you could have memories from the womb, your dad saying, "You're going to be a beautiful, loved baby" would certainly sound like "Mmphs ... girgle ... mphhss ... splosh" in the womb.

I recently heard that the 75-year-old CEO from Toyota had recalled 500,000 vehicles. I thought, "Wow, what a memory." My memory isn't that good. The only benefit is that I'm able to convince Lorraine I really was listening when she asked me to do something, but I forgot. I think I may have written about that in an earlier chapter. I don't remember.

One of my true pleasures of getting older is watching my children grow into productive adults. I have wonderful children. You always remain their parents and worry about them no matter how old they are. My own kids are in their 30s and 40s, and they still enjoy it when I read to them ... from my will. While I'll always worry about my children, I'm immensely proud that all three of them are productive, kind individuals, and all are married to wonderful, supportive spouses.

So here I sit, swatting at flies that turn out to be floaters, but pretty darn happy to be here. You're not old when you continually look forward, not back, and when you're amazed to discover and learn new things. The view from up here is good, much clearer than many occasions during the climb. Here's to many more sunrises, my friends.

CHAPTER 12

What Was Your Favorite Trip?

My son Zach recently asked about my favorite trip. I grew up during the 1960s and 1970s, a period now called "the Sixties." Consequently, I had done mind-altering psychedelic drugs many times during my misspent youth, but my most memorable trip was in 1975, when my University of Wisconsin housemates and I took LSD.

I had windowpane tabs stored in the freezer. For readers unfamiliar with LSD in the 60s, windowpane was so named because it was a very tiny transparent tab of acid. It was not much bigger than the head of a pin and had no weight or taste. Most of the guys in the house were taking acid that night, so it must have been a day of the week ending with the letters *d-a-y*.

I stood in front of the freezer, put the windowpane on the tip of my index finger, and flipped it onto my tongue from maybe an inch away. And there was the problem. I should have placed it directly onto my tongue. But I didn't. I sort of tossed it, dropped it, into my mouth. A half hour later, I wasn't feeling any effect from the acid. I wasn't tripping. My roommates were all tripping, and I wasn't. I must have missed my mouth and dropped the virtually invisible windowpane on the floor.

I returned to the freezer, got another hit of windowpane, and carefully placed it directly on my tongue. About two minutes later (you're probably way ahead of me on this story), the first hit kicked in. My memories of the evening are spotty. I know I was in the backseat of a car driven by a guy named Dick and that he stopped in the parking lot, opened his trunk, and somehow attached a set of bull horns to the hood of his car. I know we picked up Man Mountain Mike Mahalek from the Chinese restaurant where he was a dishwasher. I know we were driving on the interstate when Dick exited and told all of us that we'd been driving the wrong way. That's all I know.

The public perceptions and attitudes toward drug use continue to evolve. For me, this evolution is readily observable in my parents' views on marijuana. I'm dealing with aging parents. Don't get me wrong. I'm thrilled they're still alive and well and that, as the only adult child living within one thousand miles of them, they're able to put 100 percent of their laser-like attention on every aspect of my life.

There's a bargain that children have no role in negotiating. Parents feed and clothe you for your first 18 years, the first few of which you don't remember, and you take care of them for last years of their life, most of which they won't remember. That's the deal. You change my diapers, and I'll hire someone to change yours.

Several years ago, I went to a movie with my dad. After I paid for our tickets, staring at the ticket I had just handed him, he said, "You didn't get my senior discount." Then he asked, "Don't you get the senior discount too?" "No, Dad. I'm not 62. I'm 60," I replied. The next time we went to a movie, my dad purchased senior tickets for both of us. The last time he'd lied about my age for a movie ticket discount was when I was 15 so I could still get an "under 12" ticket. Yeah, I was short. Remember?

My folks are in their 90s now, and things, especially technology, have moved too quickly. As their world gets smaller, there are fewer activities I can do with my folks. Plays and concerts are nice, especially if there's a matinee.

My son Zach and I recently took my folks to see the Four Lads in concert. The Four Lads had a successful career 60 years earlier. Zach was the youngest person at the concert. I was the second youngest. I struggle to convey the demographics of this concert. Imagine an AARP conference in town. With that image, now imagine that everyone from the AARP conference dropped off their parents to see the Four Lads.

I digress from the topic of my parents' evolving views on marijuana. This is the story of how my mother got a medical marijuana card. After surgery on both ankles, severe arthritis often caused her to wince in pain. After trying topical ointments and painkillers, she got desperate enough to try marijuana, the medical use of which had been approved in Arizona. She had never smoked anything but a salmon. (And how she kept it lit, I'll never know.) "Lee," she said, "at this point, I really would try it. I can't do that oxycondom they give me. It makes me like a zombie."

I agreed that she ought to give it a try. Having never used tobacco, she exclaimed, "But, Lee, I could never smoke it."

I explained, "Mom, you don't have to smoke it. You can eat marijuana gummy bears."

"Really?" she asked.

"Yes, Mom, really. You should definitely try marijuana. All the cool kids are doing it. I think half the audience at the Four Lads was stoned. We could've made a lot of money with a Twinkie concession stand."

Before actually agreeing to try marijuana, she had more than a few questions: How much should I take? Can I take it with my other medication? How long does it last? Should you do it on an empty stomach? And my favorite: Can I take it with grapefruit juice?

These were all excellent questions, none of which I would have ever considered asking in my youth. My friends and I grew up on drugs. We never asked how long it would last or if we could take other drugs while we were on those drugs. The guys I could've asked about this wouldn't have known any more than I, and I didn't trust the adults who claimed they knew the answers.

In 1967, the television show *Dragnet* aired an episode called "The Big High," where a young, stoned hippie couple argues with Sgt. Joe Friday, played stoically by Jack Webb, that marijuana is harmless. Then, while stoned, the couple forgets about their baby, who drowns in their bathtub. Officers Joe Friday and Bill Gannon, played by Harry Morgan (who famously went on to play Col. Potter in *MASH*), shake their heads, hold their hats in their hands, and Gannon solemnly asks Friday:

Gannon: Joe, can you handle this for a minute?
Friday: You alright?
Gannon: First time since I've been on the job ...
Friday: Yeah.
Gannon: I think I'm gonna be sick.

Then he hands Friday the bag of weed and runs out of the room to puke. That was the message of my youth. Smoke weed, drown your kid. Everyone from age 16 up knew this was bullshit. So why ask questions when you don't trust the source of the answer? Since medical marijuana had been authorized in Arizona, I told my mom she should ask the doctor for answers when we went for her medical certification.

The medical certification examination was cursory at best. The doctor actually seemed a little miffed that my mom had brought the operative reports from her recent ankle surgeries. Having watched the medical marijuana certification procedure, I can't imagine anyone not getting approved for medical marijuana. I qualified by complaining of menstrual cramps.

After my mom was medically certified, got her card, and got her cannabis gummy bears, my 27-year-old, Zach, developed a much greater interest in grandma. Infants and children love grandma and grandpa. That fascination wanes by the time grandchildren are teenagers, not because children grow up but because grandparents grow old. Interest in your grandparents correlates exactly with the fun you have with them. Suddenly, they aren't crawling on the ground or tossing a football around or having a tea party. They're talking about all their sick or dying friends and telling the same stories over and over again, sometimes in the course of one visit. Not me. No way. When I'm a grandparent, I'm going to be fun, crazy grampa. When I hack up phlegm in the morning, we're going to have a loogie-spitting contest. (Gross, I know. But the loogie-spitting contest is actually the least disgusting thing you can do with phlegm.)

So Zach was coming by to see Grandma. I came by one afternoon and saw *The Wizard of Oz* on television but no sound coming from the TV. The 27-year-old and his 81-year-old grandma were listening to an iPod with a dual set of headphones. "Lee, what are you doing here?"

"Mom, why are you watching *The Wizard of Oz* with no sound?"

"We're listening to Dark Floyd, *The Pink Side of the Moon*. Did you know it syncs perfectly with the movie? It's like they planned it."

"Mom, are you eating gummy bears with Zach?"

"I'm not eating gummy bears. I'm eating Cheetos," she said, showing me fingertips the color of Donald Trump's spray tan.

"Dad, I didn't do any gummies. I haven't used marijuana in years."

"So you just came to watch Grandma get stoned?"

"Yeah and play some music for her. Did you know Grandma never listened to music in ear buds?"

"Lee?"

"Yes, Mom?"

"Did you know that at the end of 'Strawberry Fields Forever,' they're saying, 'I buried Paul'?"

"Actually, Mom, someone told me they really said, 'I'm

very bored.' But this is a very weird conversation."

"Lee?"

"Yes, Mom?"

"Ed Meyerson wants to get a marijuana card. Can you take him?" In the few short months after my mom got her card, I became the weed Sherpa for the entire retirement community.

After getting a few pre-rolls from my mom for driving her to the dispensary, I discovered that weed sold today is unbelievably strong. Too strong. One tiny hit and you're wasted. Two hits and you're hallucinating. The social experience of sitting in a circle and passing joints around for hours as I did in college is gone. I understand that things change. We stream music and can't read album liner notes about the musicians on a record. Or roll joints in the crease of a double album. By creating superstrains of marijuana, we've lost the social pleasure of sitting around for hours, smoking joint after joint while getting mildly stoned— stoned as much from lack of oxygen to the brain as from the THC content in the weed. That's why I anticipate pot dealers, I mean medical dispensaries, will bring back the old strains of weed from the '60s. They'll call it Acapulco Gold or Panama Red or maybe they'll just call it Shitty Pot. But I predict that at some point, they'll sell pot like we had in the 60s so we can sit in a circle and smoke it all night. Just like vinyl has returned and kids today are buying albums and reading liner notes, the return of shitty pot seems inevitable.

Whoa! Lorraine suggested that the question Zach asked about my favorite trip may have been directed at travel rather than psychedelic trips. In the unlikely event that the question was intended to elicit a different response than the one above, let me say that one of my favorite trips (travelwise) was the first time Lorraine and I went to Europe. We took a trip to Italy. It had been a long flight, with the monitor on the plane mapping our route from Atlanta to Rome. Looking around as the cabin lights came on, I noticed my fellow travelers looked like pasty, disheveled crackheads who'd gone too long without the pipe. I imagine that for those nicotine-addicted passengers, the metaphor was fairly accurate.

Lorraine and I were excited about our first trip to Europe. Our only trepidation was the result of continuous warnings we'd received from experienced travelers about pickpockets. Apparently, lots of people have visited Italy, and Lorraine and I had met all of them in the six months before our trip. They gave us all sorts of advice and suggestions. My personal favorite was when one well-meaning traveler sincerely told me, "If a pigeon craps on your head, don't wipe it off. Just let it lay there until it dries. Wiping it when it's wet just smears it all around."

Apparently, birds shitting on your head is a huge problem in Italy. This guy told me the problem is the worst at the Vatican. Maybe that's why you always see the pope in a hat. But I'm fully prepared to stand with my head covered in bird turd while I wait for it to dry. No problem.

To a person, everyone who had visited Italy or knew anyone who had ever visited Italy warned us about pickpockets. My mom, who had never even been to Venice Beach, California, warned us about pickpockets. So pickpockets became a cause of anxiety about the trip. "Well-dressed businessmen will distract you while their partner picks your pocket," we were told. Or "Hordes of gypsy children will swarm you and pick your pockets." Finally, based on a *Golden Girls* rerun, my mom insisted, "Women holding what appears to be a baby will throw it at you so when you catch what is actually a doll, they can pick your pocket." Based on this well-meaning advice, I was prepared to be rude to businessmen, run from children faster than David Duke at a Juneteenth celebration, and dodge any thrown babies. These had to be the worst people on the planet. Well, maybe not the worst. I suppose the worst would throw real babies at us. But darn close.

When we took the shuttle from the airport to our hotel, our driver pointed out various sites and then told us with no small degree of pride that pickpockets from all over the world came to ply their trade in Rome. I imagined some small-town Romanian pickpocket getting up one morning, inspired by Frank Sinatra, and singing, "If I can make it there, I can make it anywhere" and then making his way to Rome. My imagination really went wild over the field day I knew that these little thieves would have with me. Like a magician who pulls some poor sap from the audience and later hands him his polka-dot boxer shorts, I would surely be that sap. No sooner would I try to spot the guy who took my passport than some baby-throwing, smiling businessman would be rifling through my wallet, surrounded by gypsy children waving my polka-dot boxers.

We took it easy our first day in Rome and ended the day with dinner and gelato. My favorite part of the dinner was the very simple and delicious bruschetta (toasted bread with tomato, olive oil, basil, salt, and pepper). That was it. On Saturday, we woke for our trip to the Vatican museum. The taxi cost ten euros. We paid to be able to jump the line to get inside without waiting for hours. While waiting to go in, we were told that photographs couldn't be taken inside the Sistine Chapel because of a Japanese company's trademark. No shit. The Japanese have a trademark on the Sistine Chapel. The line to get in for those who didn't pay to skip it was blocks long. No idea if it's always like that or if it was just because it was the Sunday before Easter. While waiting, I scanned the sky for pigeons. All clear. When we got to the Sistine Chapel, people routinely violated the rule and took pictures. And you know who were the worst offenders? The Japanese. Like they own the place. You might think I'm stereotyping people, but the Japanese took a shitload of pictures.

As we headed through the maze leading to the chapel, we went through room after room of murals, tapestries, and painted ceilings. After scouring the skies for pigeons and staring up at the ceiling for hours, I decided some clever entrepreneur could make a few euros with a chiropractor concession outside the Vatican museum. The museum and the chapel were cool. If you like Catholic stuff, Italy is the place for you. One thing that was interesting is how rich people got themselves in paintings with Jesus. The Medici family was really rich and ruled over a lot of Italy. So when they would commission a famous painter to do a picture of Jesus and the Virgin Mary, they'd tell the painter to put them in the picture. Yep, there's Jesus and Mary and Joseph. And that wise man? That's Mr. Medici. Honest to God. All the rich guys who commissioned painters to do religious paintings (and that's the only kind of paintings we saw) had the artist stick them or their family in the picture as a wise man or a king or whatever. I don't see why it was such a big deal. I Photoshop my head on a picture with Elvis and the pope all the time. But back then, people didn't use Photoshop. So they just stuck themselves in Jesus paintings they commissioned. Just like my great-great-grandkids will think I was good friends with Elvis Presley and the pope, people today walk through the Sistine Chapel, see the paintings, and say, "Wow, the Medicis were the three wise men."

We next took a taxi to the Seven Steps. Lorraine was impressed with how the Romans had fit their modern city among the old buildings and winding roads. I was most impressed that we weren't killed in a car crash in the cab. After dinner, we walked to the Plaza Navona and the Trevi Fountain. We were told the fountain was for lovers, but this could be a myth as no one was making love in the fountain. The next day, we toured the Coliseum. Amazing history. The Coliseum was built in 80 AD, held 65,999 people, and had assigned seats with your name engraved in the stones. Fabrics were anchored from outside to the inside of the arena to provide shade. Gladiators and animals entered from beneath the stage through a pulley system. It was really fascinating.

Italy was a lot of fun, and if you go, you've already read about the pigeons and pickpockets, so here are a few additional tips I'm happy to pass along. First, apparently the warnings on Italian cigarette packages say that smoking is good for you as most everyone does it. Hotels in Rome have a little toddler sink next to the toilet, which makes you wish you were two years old. Coffee is more expensive if you order while you're sitting at a table than if you get it at the counter and drink it there. If you're asked if you want water and say yes, you have to pay for that water. Little kids will talk to you in Italian, which is very weird. A small can of Coke costs more than a bottle of wine. Seats are assigned on trains. Finally, you shouldn't drive in Rome unless you have some NASCAR experience. There are whole neighborhoods where you can't drive without a permit. And if you don't read Italian, you won't know you've entered these forbidden zones. If you drive in those neighborhoods without a permit, the Italians give you two tickets, one when you enter the forbidden zone and one when you leave. When we returned to the United States, we got fines from an Italian court that tracked down our address through the rental car company. That's right. Italian law enforcement will mail you collection letters for those tickets after you're back home. If that experience has happened to anyone reading this and you've ever gone back to Italy, please contact me and let me know if you were arrested at the border or when you tried renting a car. Unless someone calls me and gives me the all-clear sign, I'm not going back to Italy.

Here's a picture of me and Lorraine in Italy ... I think.

CHAPTER 13

Do You Have Any Family Stories to Share?

No matter how old we are, as long as our parents are alive, we're still their children. We can be on Medicare, but we're still their children. My mom and dad are in their 90s. Last night we had dinner, and a friend stopped by and briefly met them. Afterward he told me how sharp and "with it" my parents were. I found that encouraging. To be considered sharp and "with it" in your 90s is apparently a very low bar. Having awareness of current events, not drooling, and just being able to string words together into sentences appear to be the only prerequisites. In all candor, both my mom and dad are very sharp in their nineties. They stay current on local, national and world events, have a good social life, and people are rightfully impressed that they are both "with it".

My 90-year-old mother grew up in a world where having a phone was a big deal, a time when long-distance calls were so prohibitively expensive that you had to quickly pass the phone around so everyone could say "hello" but not stay on too long to have any meaningful conversation because of the rates. (Sunday rates were cheaper, so that was a good day to talk to Uncle Oscar in Minneapolis.) My mom must still think it costs a lot to call long distance. This is the only explanation I can come up with as to why she wants me to

71

call relatives when I'm visiting the city where they live.

Last year, I went to Boston. My cousin Jeannie lives there. We're not particularly close. I haven't seen or talked to her since my bar mitzvah. I'm not even friends with her on Facebook, and I have friends on Facebook whom I've never met. As I was leaving for Boston, my mom said, "You should call your cousin Jeannie."

I told her, "Mom, I'm not going to see her when I go to Boston."

She said, "I know. That's okay. But you should call her."

"Why?" I asked.

And she said, "Because you're right there. You're in Boston. You should call her." I haven't spoken to my cousin Jeannie in more than 45 years. Explaining to my mom that it makes no more sense for me to call her because we're in the same area code runs contrary to the laws of the universe. The earth revolves around the sun, right? Well, there you go. If you're in Boston, you have to call your cousin Jeannie.

And so I did. In what was clearly as uncomfortable a phone call for her as it was for me, let me give you my side of the conversation.

"Hi, Jeannie. This is your cousin Elliot. Yes, I know. It has been a really long time ... Yeah, not since my bar mitzvah ... No, my face cleared up. Yeah, it was pretty bad when I was a kid ... Well, I just wanted to call you to tell you I'm in Boston ... No, I won't see you while I'm here ... That's right ... Because my mom wanted me to, that's why ... Well, maybe she wanted you to know that while I haven't seen you for the last 45 years from two thousand miles away, now I won't see you from much closer. (Long, awkward pause) Bye."

From the day I was born to this day, my mom has been very protective of me. "Don't punish Elliot," she would tell my teacher every year on the first day of school. "Punish the boy next to him. My son will get the message."

My dad expressed his love differently. When I was 11, he sent me out on Halloween night covered from head to toe in black. "Lee, this Halloween you're going out in a black shirt, black pants, and black tennis shoes. You're the Dark Goblin."

"Dad, great. What's the Dark Goblin's superpower?"

"The Dark Goblin will be completely invisible ... to cars!" My dad was a funny guy. Well, guess what? The Dark Goblin wound up having a great night and coming home with a ton of candy. Sure, cars hit me, just clipped me mostly. But I got a lot of what I call "don't call the cops candy." Trust me, when a driver wings you, you pretty much get all the candy in the car. I remember coming home from my Dark Goblin night. Dad was surprised when I returned home with so much candy. Frankly, he was surprised I returned home at all.

All-you-can-eat Friday fish fries were a favorite of my family and of most families in Milwaukee. Every restaurant had, and most still have, a Friday night fish fry. Back then it was an all-you-can-eat affair. The Glicksmans had a game plan going into these meals. Eat the fish. Not the potatoes. Not the rolls. Not even the coleslaw. Just the fish. Every week, if my dad and my grandfather saw me eating a side dish, they'd invariably shout across the table, "Don't fill up on the rolls. Put down the potato. You eat that and they're making money on you!" It wasn't that my folks were cheap or that we stuffed food into our pockets. They just wanted their money's worth.

I have no doubt that 1960s restaurants bear much of the blame for the current obesity crisis. The portions became enormous, and so did we. We're all supersized. The smorgasbords and all-you-can-eat specials were common, not just at fish fries but at many restaurants.

"Welcome to Tivoli" (which, the menu proudly proclaimed, was backward for 'I love it"). "Are you here for the all-you-can-eat fish fry?" You're kidding, right? All you can eat? That's not a description. That's a challenge! To all the men of my parents' generation, me, and all my friends, "all you can eat" was really asking, "How much can you eat?" And trust me, you can eat a lot as long as you don't fill up on the rolls and potatoes. Whenever we went to an all-you-can-eat buffet, my response was to eat like Joey Chestnut on the Fourth of July.

Over time, I don't think restaurants became concerned about their contribution to nationwide obesity as much as the fact that they were losing money. I'm surprised how long it actually took for restaurants to realize that in our ultracompetitive society, it probably wasn't a good idea to issue the all-you-can-eat challenge anymore. Of course, I'm also surprised it took so long to put wheels on luggage or cupholders in cars (which, by the way, are the two greatest innovations of my lifetime). Anyway, restaurants now have what they call "all you care to eat." This allows everyone not from Mississippi to have an out when they don't go back for thirds. "Hey, I could eat more. Absolutely I could eat more, but you know what, buddy? Maybe I just don't care to."

———

Why did I just pick on Mississippi? I'm from Wisconsin, where cheese and sausage rule. In terms of obesity, my home state is the wurst, right? No. No, Wisconsin is actually not the fattest state. We have other distinctions. According to a Daily Beast story of June 29, 2015, we're the state that drinks the most alcohol. One news source concluded that Wisconsin had half of the 20 "drunkest" cities in America. Per capita, Wisconsin may also have the most serial killers, with two of the top three having also eaten their victims. But, apparently, Jeffrey Dahmer and Ed Gein didn't overindulge. They both looked well-proportioned and weight appropriate. In any event, Wisconsin isn't even in the top ten for obesity. Number one on the chunky chart really does goes to Mississippi, where, in 2013, over 35 percent of the population self-reported as being obese. *Self-reported* means "underreported." I've driven through Mississippi, and I estimate 90 percent of the folks there are sumo wannabes.

CHAPTER 14

Do You Keep in Touch with Many High School Friends?

I don't keep in touch with many friends from high school because I never had many friends in high school. In January 1968, we moved from the inner city of Milwaukee, where I attended Peckham Junior High, which later became Jackie Robinson Middle School, and, even later, closed. It was a very tough school. The school was a mixture of black kids and white greasers. Our yearbook had student photos in front and profile. The school newspaper had an obituary page. You get the idea.

Growing up, my parents insisted that I needed a good education to survive in the world. Nancy and Dave Glicksman stressed the importance of education. As a young boy, I remember them saying repeatedly and unconvincingly that they didn't care what I did as long as I did my best at whatever it was I did. "Lee, we don't care what you do as long as you do your best. If you're a ditchdigger, that's fine. Just be the best ditchdigger you can be!" But in point of fact, at a very early age, I knew they really didn't want me to be a ditchdigger, even if I was the undisputed world's best ditchdigger. They wanted me to go to college, something neither of them had done.

My parents insisted I had very few options if I didn't go

to college. One option actually: ditchdigger. The fork in the road pointed in only two directions, as they explained it: ditchdigger or college. "You need to get an education. You're not going to be a ditchdigger. Not with your asthma. There's not a big need for a four-foot-six-inch asthmatic ditchdigger." I never knew any ditchdiggers, and as far as I could tell, neither did my parents.

The implication was that there were these guys who dug ditches deep into the earth using nothing more than their brute strength and a shovel. In my mother's dystopian vision of my future, there were no other tools or machinery available for the digging of said ditches. Apparently, in her Mad Max, postapocalyptic worldview, there were no backhoes or anything motorized. It didn't take long before I realized there were no ditchdiggers, at least not the type they were suggesting I'd have to become. At least, I'd never seen one, and I'm quite sure they hadn't either. Trust me, if there had been people who really grabbed shovels and dug ditches, I would've heard about it. "Look, Lee. Look. See that guy in the ditch shoveling out rocks? Look down. It's just his head sticking above the street. That's another ditchdigger."

But a good lesson for parents is that when you start making stuff up, even with good intentions of scaring your kids into getting an education, sooner or later they'll figure it out and start to wonder how much other stuff is true. That's why everyone my age smoked weed. As soon as one of your friends tried it, you learned that all the stuff your parents told you about it was bullshit and just designed to scare you into not trying it. Every parent said smoking weed made you crazy in a bad psychotic way, not in a fun "wow, this is crazy" way.

Early on, I realized the choice of either college or ditchdigger was a false one. As soon as some of my friends began smoking weed, I realized parental preaching, though well-intentioned, was uninformed. It took a while, but over time, my parents learned they had been misled by a propaganda campaign against marijuana. Fast forward to 2014, when, after three separate ankle surgeries, my 81-year-old mother got her medical marijuana card. On her first trip to the dispensary, she got a pre-roll, which is apparently a medical term for a joint, and gave it to me.

Back to why I had few high school friends. It was a restless time in Milwaukee, Wisconsin. Racial tensions were high, culminating in the "Long Hot Summer of 1967", a summer when the riots over racial inequality swept the country. Milwaukee wasn't spared. Riots took place near our house. Some people died. Curfews were imposed. Like the Old Testament Jews who put lambs' blood on their doors so the angel of death would pass over when God inflicted plagues on the Egyptians for enslaving the Jews, businesses put "soul brother" signs in their windows, hoping that rioters and looters would similarly pass over their property. Italian pizza parlors, Polish bakeries, and Jewish delicatessens posted signs exclaiming "soul brother." My grandfather and uncle owned a tavern in the heart of the city. They didn't need a sign. The Wisconsin National Guard was deployed with rifles across the street from the tavern.

I really thought I was friends with and knew everything about everyone in my class at Peckham Junior High in the spring of 1967. Apparently not. One weekday in 1967, while in seventh grade, at exactly 11:30 the black students suddenly stood up and walked out. Every single black student in unison. Although I had a mix of black and white friends with whom I rode to school on the city bus, I knew nothing about the walkout before it happened. Why wasn't I in on this?

My parents were concerned about the violence erupting around us. At Peckham, I got beat up. A lot. I could've made a couple extra bucks on Saturdays for kids' birthday parties as a piñata, but then there would have been no way to distinguish weekends from my school days.

Given my stature and decided lack of speed, I couldn't

avoid getting into and losing fights. Fearing for my safety and concerned about the quality of education, my parents moved to a suburban town they could barely afford so my sisters and I could get a quality education and they could save money on bandages. We moved to Whitefish Bay (or White Folks Bay, as it was often called).

The village of Whitefish Bay was preppy before the word *preppy* existed. Blue jeans were not allowed in middle school. For that matter, blue jeans weren't allowed in high school until the great Whitefish Bay High protest in the spring of 1969. Yeah, while the City of Milwaukee was in flames over housing discrimination and kids were shutting down college campuses over the Vietnam War, at Whitefish Bay High, the kids took on the big issues: did the rivets on the back of our jeans really scratch desk chairs, or was this just a bunch of bullshit passed down from the Man?

I walked into the back of the homeroom class on the first day of the spring semester of eighth grade. The teacher cleared her throat and introduced me from her podium. Heads turned, and everyone looked to see a four-foot-six-inch greaser from the city. Most of the students had grown up in the Bay and had known each other since kindergarten. Wearing a sweater that my mother had knitted with a big P patch on it, because I had been on the Peckham Junior High gymnastics team, I felt as welcome as Kanye West at a bar mitzvah.

No one else was wearing a letter sweater. Hadn't these kids watched *Leave It to Beaver*? I thought all white suburban rich kids wore letter sweaters. Kids stared, looked at one another, and some, under their breath, mumbled. Then they all turned back to the front of the class and ignored me. Between classes, during the lunch hour, and after school, not one student said a word to me.

Fitting in was, putting it mildly, a challenge. Trying to look tough at Peckham in seventh grade, I wore skin-tight black Levi's, had my hair slicked back, and wore black shoes that came to a point. I was four feet, six inches tall. I didn't look tough. I looked like a cross between Elvis and a Keebler elf. Thinking it would toughen my image, I'd put a toothpick in my mouth. The toothpick didn't make me look tough. It made me look like an appetizer. "Hey, cool it, pal. You heard me. Cool it! You don't want any of this. You bend over, and I'll poke your eye out. Bend lower. No, a little lower." At the time, with a toothpick clenched between my teeth like a tiny ice pick, I thought I looked tough. In hindsight, I looked as threatening as a Lollipop Guild member.

So we moved to Whitefish Bay, where my only eighth-grade report card read:

Social Studies: C
English: D
Science: F
Math: F

My reputation heading into high school for ninth grade had been set. I was no longer the short greaser kid I was when I arrived. I was now the short, *dumb* greaser kid. Okay, so maybe as a kid, one of my insecurities was my height. That incident, to make a long story only slightly longer, is why I had few friends in high school.

I am no longer friends with anyone from Whitefish Bay High School. My best friend in high school was George. We spent days together listening to 45s and record albums, trying to meet girls, riding our bikes and later joyriding in cars. We were like brothers. I would have taken a bullet for George. (I would not have taken a rifle for him as it would have been way too hard to conceal.)

High school ended in 1972, over 50 years ago. Over the intervening years, it became clear that our political views were diametrically opposed. Some may ask, "Can't you put aside politics and remain close friends?" However, that's really impossible. My views on healthcare, the environment, the right to choose, gun-safety laws, and immigration are all part of my politics. We have little to discuss other than sports or family. Sadly, we're more Facebook acquaintances, wishing each other a happy birthday, than true friends. I still love the guy and would do anything for him. I just wish we had more in common than memories.

I'd be remiss if I didn't mention the one person from high school with whom I remained friends until his untimely death from pancreatic cancer in March 2006 at the age of 51: Mike Mahalek. I met Mike in the fall of 1968. We were freshmen in high school. We had a lot in common. We were both under five feet tall and weighed less than one hundred pounds. We had other stuff in common. We both had asthma. This was a time when inhalers had just been invented. Mike called it his "goose juice." We'd often go by each other's house to borrow a spray. Our asthma was frequently brought on by laughter. We'd go to the Bay Shore strip mall, eat a cream puff at Grebe's Bakery, start laughing, and need a spray

We lived together in Madison in 1975. I was a student. Mike was working. One night, we both took a tab of LSD and wound up walking for what seemed like hours in a horrible rainstorm. We returned home, soaked to the skin, and both of us were in desperate need of a bathroom. Doing what guys have done as long as there have been toilets, we stood side by side at the john and peed. Nothing weird. No sword fight. We just peed. Then, soaked from the rain, I shivered. When I shivered, some drops sprayed Mike. "You pissed on me! Glicksman, I can't believe you pissed on me!" "No," I protested, "that was just rain shaking off my hair." For the next 30 years, Mike often reminded me that I'd pissed on him. I continued to tell him it was rain.

Another thing we had in common was our athletic prowess or lack thereof. We had a gym class together, and in the swimming class, they separated the students into groups, depending on their ability. One group was the "sharks." These were the guys who could swim effortlessly in the pool, lap after lap. The next group was the "minnows." These guys could also swim, but they needed some instruction.

Mike and I had our own little group. We were the "rocks."

Our swim instructor's teaching technique was to push us into the deep end of the pool, where Mike and I would cling to the sides, shivering, for 45 minutes. And that's how I got to know Mike, holding on to the side of the pool, shivering. He looked like a chihuahua. Mike grew. I didn't.

In 2005, Mike was diagnosed with pancreatic cancer. He died nine months after his diagnosis. I sent him a joke on a postcard by mail every day from August 2005 until the day he died on March 19, 2006. I spent five or six days with him the month before he died. We took a walk together. He said he couldn't have had a better friend and leaned over and kissed the top of my forehead. I told him I was sorry that I had peed on him.

It was frustrating being thousands of miles from my best friend. Daily postcards with a joke was one way I'd hoped I could give him ten seconds every day of respite. I also called Christine Nuernberg, the mayor of Mequon, Wisconsin, and asked if she could do me a favor. I told her one of her most decent residents was dying and that I was coming in to visit him in February 2016. I asked if she could designate one of the days of my visit as Mike Mahalek Day in the town of Mequon, Wisconsin. She graciously agreed, and one day in February 2006, the town of Mequon celebrated Mike Mahalek Day. I would've loved to have read the proclamation, but I knew I'd never be able to read it without breaking down. I cried once in front of Mike about his situation and vowed to myself it would not happen again. I wouldn't be sad and put my best friend, who was dying, in a position of having to comfort me. So our mutual friend Doug Eiring read the proclamation announcing Mike Mahalek Day as Mike sat in his living room hooked up to an IV.

The following day, cards and letters began to come in from people all over the country wishing Mike a "Happy Mike Mahalek Day." Some cards were funny. "Our traditional Mike Mahalek Day dinner is borscht and shepherd's pie." Or "My family always waits for the day-after Mike Mahalek

Day shopping deals." I loved it because Mike loved it.

I never saw Mike cry or complain after he was diagnosed with a death sentence, except once. When his oldest son, John, who was away for his freshman year at the University of Montana, called and told his dad about a great beer he had tried. Mike smiled and said, "We'll have to drink one of those sometime." His voice was clear and strong, but tears streamed down his face as he said it.

On the Sunday I left Wisconsin the month before Mike died, he was weak. He was mostly chair-bound. Mike was tired; we'd done a lot, had a lot of fun, and we'd celebrated Mike Mahalek Day. Mike sat in his chair, and we hugged. I turned around and began to leave, knowing I'd never see him again. Mike got up, stood behind me, and gave me a hug. As he hugged me, he said, "I love you," and I said, "I love you." And we were crying, and he was behind me, hugging me, and we were both saying, "I love you." Then I said, "This looks like a trailer for *Brokeback Mountain*." And we started laughing. And that's how I left him. Laughing and crying. And we didn't need our goose juice.

I gave Mike's eulogy. I started with a joke: "When I saw Mike in the casket, it just didn't look like him. His glasses were clean, and they were on straight." I needed to pause a couple times, had a catch in my voice once or twice. But I didn't cry.

Me and Mike Mahalek in the summer of 2005

CHAPTER 15

What Was Your First Job?

I remember first receiving money when I was in seventh grade. In the spring of 1967, my friend Jerry Volkin and I took public transportation to an upscale Milwaukee suburb called Whitefish Bay. We walked along the tony houses on Lake Drive, raising money for our scout troop. We answered questions about how the funds would be used and told them of our admiration for our scoutmaster. People were very generous, especially considering we weren't even wearing our scout uniforms. Jerry and I never had Boy Scout uniforms, not because we were too poor to own them but because we were not in the Boy Scouts.

The first time I was paid for something legitimate was when I babysat the Right boys. Mrs. Right was divorced and had three somewhat unruly sons. She wanted a boy to babysit. In the fall of 1968, I was a freshman in high school, and I babysat them a couple days a week after school. Since I've never checked the Wisconsin inmate population, I'm going to assume they turned out well. The pay was adequate, especially if you included the vodka I replaced with water. Mrs. Right had to have known her vodka had been replaced by a liquid with the same alcohol content as Lake Michigan. I'm guessing she felt it was a small price to pay for finding a guy who'd babysit.

After reading these last paragraphs, I guess you have a pretty good impression of me in my youth. If you do, I'd love to see it. I used to do impressions. In grade school, I was on *Amateur Showcase* on WTMJ in Milwaukee, which sounds like a television station started by dentists. I did the Ed Sullivan Show, where I imitated Ed, Louis Armstrong, Crazy Guggenheim, and Don Adams as Maxwell Smart. The principal of the 38th Street School was so impressed by my impressions that he let me go from class to class one day doing my show for all the students. I then got to be on *Kids Club,* another TV show on WTMJ. I wasn't paid for these appearances, so they weren't my first jobs.

After a brief stint at El Taco, wrapping tortillas around some kind of meat, I got my first real job at the age of 15 at the Pfister Hotel in Milwaukee, working on the banquet floor. I earned $2.73 an hour plus tips. The tips were good, often doubling my salary. In that job, I was a 15-year-old labor union member. From 1970 to 1972, I was also the only white bar porter at the Pfister Hotel in Milwaukee. After living in the City of Milwaukee, it had been a shock to move to that same Whitefish Bay suburb where I'd raised money for a fictitious scout troop and attend a school where every kid in my class was white and, in my view, full of themselves.

I had many interesting jobs because, to have money, I needed to work. I bussed tables at the Iron Horse restaurant in Milwaukee, mopped floors at the University of Wisconsin-Whitewater, flipped burgers at the Hardees in Whitewater, and spent summers as a camp counselor. I sold shoes and dancewear in Madison, Wisconsin, and after moving to Tucson, I got a decent paying job as a law clerk. From 15 until the age of 67, I always had a job, except when I started law school. In the summer of 1976, I moved to Tucson to attend law school in the fall. I arrived in Tucson with a suitcase, a duffel bag, and something less than $2,000 in my pocket. When I arrived in the Old Pueblo, I knew no one in Arizona.

Exiting the airport, it was as though I'd walked into a blast furnace. My face began melting off like the Nazi in the first Indiana Jones movie. A Yellow Cab was stopped with a reflective sunshield in its windshield. I'm sure it kept the cab cooler, but I have to think it made driving difficult. Rolling down the driver's side window with his head stuck out to see where he was going, the driver took me into town. Sunburnt-face Yellow Cab guy dropped me off with my duffel bag and suitcase at the law school. Without a car, I needed to live within walking distance of the school. Having no idea where anything was, but assuming the campus was surrounded by student housing, I headed south. In the hundred-plus-degree weather, I went about four blocks, found an apartment I couldn't afford, and set down roots.

I was determined not to have a job my first semester of law school. If I flunked out, I didn't want to have the excuse of not having had enough time to study. In the summer of 1976, up until the time classes began, I donated plasma twice a week: $15 for the first donation, $25 for the second. Forty bucks a week helped. I didn't have much money when I started law school, hardly enough for a social life. In law school, I needed to make friends quickly. I once approached a longhaired law student in the library and asked, "Hey, do you want to get high?"

When he excitedly replied, "Yes," I said, "Great. Do you have any weed?" I made several friends this way and got stoned a lot. I don't remember who any of them were, but they were nice.

After my first semester of law school, having received all Cs, I could no longer go without working. I needed a job. Outside of my classmates, I knew no one in Tucson. I spent a day taking the elevator to the top floor of each downtown building with a stack of resumés in my backpack and knocked on doors trying to find clerking work. With just one semester of law school and only C grades, lawyers were not eager to hire me. I got three offers out of over 70 offices, one from a previously disbarred lawyer, another from an aging bullshit artist of a lawyer, and one from William

Urban. I'm pretty sure his receptionist felt sorry for me and made Urban see me. For whatever reason, he offered me a job. I worked for him throughout law school until I graduated in May 1979. Maybe being around a lawyer and reading materials written by a real lawyer helped me better understand the law because in my second semester of law school, I got straight As.

Before leaving the topic of jobs, I want to bring up the best job I ever had: camp counselor. It was "the sixties." Life was simple. My favorite times growing up were going to summer camp. I didn't realize it was a Jewish camp. I just thought it was a camp for short, uncoordinated kids. Camp Timberlane was a boys' camp on 270 acres of property just north of Minocqua, Wisconsin, located on Lake Towanda. Waterfront activities included swimming, sailing, canoeing, and waterskiing. The camp even had a waterski team, the Timber Bats, which performed at other camps.

Jews send their kids to camps, which is somewhat weird because any sentence containing the words *Jews* and *camps* hasn't been positive for 75 years. Nevertheless, going to overnight camp is very much a Jewish thing. I went for nine out of 10 summers (I missed the one in 1968, when I had to go to summer school after getting two Fs in my second semester of eighth grade. You read about that in the previous chapter.)

Boys became men at summer camp. And they did so by themselves in their bunk beds. Campers were told stories of a prior camper named Neville Flange, who came to camp with a footlocker full of knives and roamed the woods around camp every summer in search of new young victims. The campers were sure Neville Flange was fake—pretty sure, anyway.

Being a camper was fun, really fun. But being a camp counselor at Camp Timberlane for Boys was the best of summers, although sticking around to help with the girls' gymnastics camp after the boys went home wasn't a bad gig either. (See the attached photo proudly displaying my

Law school, 1976

Porter Girls Gymnastics Camp shirt.) Oddly enough, parents who almost certainly wouldn't trust me to drive their car entrusted me with the care of their sons for an entire summer.

As a camp counselor, my only job was to make sure the campers had fun. I figured if I was having fun, they would too. So I had fun. All overnight camps have campfires and ghost stories like the one about Neville Flange, but I devised far more creative methods for making their summer memorable. Benny Larch was the senior counselor, and I was his counselor in training.

As an aside, has anyone else noticed that guys keep their childhood names forever? Benjamin Larch will always be Benny. My poker buddies Scott, Robert, and Michael are Scottie, Lewdog, and Mikey. Women don't keep their childhood nicknames. I think it's because it has always been more difficult for women in the workforce to be taken seriously. Men have a presumption of competence based solely on gender. It's just a theory, but I think girls called Patty or Debbie growing up become Patricia and Deborah when they begin their careers in an effort to be taken seriously.

Back to that camp counselor gig. Benny and I had the youngest, smallest campers—boys ages seven to nine. I assumed I was always put with the youngest campers because Harold Hiken, Timberlane's owner, feared that the older campers, all of whom were bigger than me, wouldn't respect my authority. These boys were at camp for a four-week or an eight-week session. At camp, these boys grew up. Most campers, probably over 80 percent, returned each summer. With each passing summer, these young boys became independent, learned to cuss and coexist with others, and learned about girls, sports, and music.

My favorite prank was called "the sun burned out." One evening, after returning from a night off, Benjamin Larch and I woke up a young camper, who came from a wealthy Chicago family. He had started the summer very disrespectful to staff, as though we were servants. He was spoiled. Or maybe that's how he always smelled. At midnight, we woke him.

"Robbie, wake up. wake up. Do you know what time it is?"

"No," he replied, wiping the sleep from his eyes.

"Robbie, you have to help us. It's 8 a.m., and the sun has burned out!"

"Huh?" he responded, now wide awake.

"Yeah, Robbie, listen. It's eight in the morning, and it's still dark outside because the sun has burned out."

At this point, Robbie was awake and maybe shaking slightly. We explained that we woke him because he was a leader in the cabin, and we wanted his help in telling the other campers. In truth, we did want his help because 1) we didn't think we could do it with a straight face, and 2) a fellow camper crying while telling the other kids would be more plausible.

One by one, we went to the other bunks, waking each

boy and telling them, with Robbie crying and confirming it was true, that the sun had burned out. We explained to the whole cabin that we were going to try to get them all back to their parents before the earth grew cold and we all froze to death. We marched the kids over to the lodge and fed them breakfast. We then told them it was a joke. Robbie said, "I knew it. I knew it wasn't true."

My last year as a camp counselor in 1975. Many of the campers whom I'd had when they were nine were now 14 and 15 years old.

I understand that times change and that if I did this today, I would probably be reported to child protective services. But none of those boys became serial killers. Yeah, some of them needed counseling, and one didn't speak for a few months. But little or no permanent harm was done. On the contrary, the following summer, at one point or another, all the boys from the 1971 Chippewa cabin, including Robbie, approached me and asked, "Are you going to do the sun burning out again this summer?" On reflection, maybe I can understand why parents wouldn't trust me to drive their car.

Chapter 16

What Were Your College Years Like?

I was born on August 23, 1954. I was a Virgo … at least until I went to college. On my 18th birthday, my parents drove me to the University of Wisconsin-Whitewater, the same school briefly attended by John Belushi. While today it is almost unthinkable that anyone would attend college without ever having seen the campus, that didn't seem unusual in 1972. The only reason I went to Whitewater, a small four-year college with perhaps 12,000 students, was because my best friend in high school indicated he was going there.

George never attended Whitewater, and when I arrived on campus on my 18th birthday, I knew no one. The drinking age in Wisconsin had been lowered to 18 with the reasoning that if kids could be drafted to fight and die in Vietnam, they ought to be allowed to drink. In 1971, with that same rationale, the voting age was lowered from 21 to 18.

I was dropped off at Wells Hall and looked forward to going to a bar for the first time … at least for the first time legally. I had no idea who my roommate was as he had not yet arrived. I didn't know anyone on campus and had no idea how to find a bar. Without a car and not knowing the direction or distance to downtown, the idea of wandering around looking for a bar was even more depressing than lying on my bed and going to sleep at 9 pm. I slept well but wondered if Whitewater had been a mistake.

The next day, my roommate, Lester Conningsby "Boz" Boseman II, the son of a successful Chicago businessman, arrived. He was cooler than I was. That wasn't just my opinion. It was his too. In fairness, nearly everyone was cooler than I was. But one of the great things about going away to college or moving anywhere is the opportunity to reinvent yourself. I could be whoever I wanted. Having had an unsatisfying high school experience, I looked forward to a fresh start. Boz was a good roommate. He was the life of the party and had a confident way about him. Unlike me, he'd actually dated while in high school and was comfortable talking to and flirting with women. Boz and I smoked marijuana daily, usually many times a day.

As an aside, here I am, 50 years later, never having dreamed that in my lifetime, I'd see a day when marijuana was legal in a number of states. I was blown away the first time I entered a weed dispensary and saw a chart listing dozens of strains of marijuana. It was like the periodic table of elements from my high school chemistry class, if the periodic table of elements had actually been something useful. In dispensaries, there are actually charts listing various types of marijuana; colorful columns of sativas, indicas, and hybrids with names like Blue Dream, Moon Walk, and Space Berry. Creators of seedless watermelons, peacharines, and grapples have nothing on the mad weed geneticists who have created strains so powerful that one toke wastes you.

One tiny hit and your lungs fill with smoke, and the smoke expands and fills your lungs like ... well, like thick expanding smoke in your lungs. Fine. I've never gotten the knack of analogies.

With all my marijuana consumption, I was surprised when my first semester grades were four Bs and one A. For the very first time in my life, I thought I could get into a law school. While classes were easy, college life during my freshman year had its difficulties. To have enough weed for our personal consumption, Boz Boseman and I would buy a pound of weed, break it up into 16 one-ounce bags, and sell 14 or 15, keeping one or two for ourselves.

One day, a guy approached Boz about buying some reefer. Boz should have been alerted when the guy never smoked it. He'd open the bag, smell it, say it smelled like "good stuff," pay for it, and leave. This transaction repeated several times over the next few weeks until one day the University of Wisconsin-Whitewater campus police showed up at our dorm room and arrested Boz.

Boz was handcuffed and perp walked down the floor of Wells Hall. A lot of conservative farm boys attended Whitewater and lived in our wing of the dorm. Many of them had been furious over the marijuana odor coming from our room despite our efforts to conceal it with air freshener, or stop it from wafting into the hall by putting a wet towel under our door. Many cheered as Boz was led away in handcuffs. Eventually, the case against Boz was resolved as a fairly minor matter, but Boz left the university after that semester.

After my first year in Wells Hall, I moved to Fischer Hall, a coed dorm. Women were on the first floor, men on the second, and so on. Access between the floors was unrestricted. Women became less mysterious and more approachable.

My grades continued to improve over my four semesters at Whitewater, so much so that I applied to University of Wisconsin-Madison. There have always been many University of Wisconsin campuses. Currently, there are 13 four-year colleges littered throughout Wisconsin, including Whitewater, Platteville, Stevens Point, Oshkosh, Milwaukee, Eau Claire, La Crosse, and Green Bay. But when you said you attended college at "Wisconsin," it meant only one place: Madison, Madtown, Mad City.

There were two reasons I didn't attend Madison immediately after high school. Number one, I wasn't smart enough. The other, at least indirectly, was the Vietnam War.

My roommate Bill Herbes and I in our Fischer Hall dorm at the UW-Whitewater. Probably should have gone with vertical stripes to look taller.

In 1969, antiwar protests at the Mifflin Street block party in Madison resulted in dozens of people injured and more than 100 arrested. During this protest, police deployed tear gas and billy clubs.

Shortly after the Mifflin Street protests, the term *billy club* fell out of favor. Maybe it sounded too violent, and police wanted a softer image than the term *billy club* conjured up. For a while, *billy clubs* were called nightsticks and now batons. Batons? Really? Let's bring back *billy club*. Police are not drum majors, and their weapon isn't used to lead a marching band. Until you show me body cam videos of officers leading criminals to a squad car while raising their baton up and down with one hand and holding a whistle in the other, I'm calling them *billy clubs*.

On August 24, 1970, at the height of the Vietnam War protests, and while I was still in high school, four young men set off an explosion in Sterling Hall, the Army Math building. The bomb went off at 3:42 am with the thought that the building would be unoccupied. Tragically, a researcher named Robert Fassnacht was working late and was killed in the blast. The four men—Karl Armstrong, Dwight Armstrong, David Fine, and Leo Burt—became fugitives and were on the FBI's most-wanted list. The Armstrong brothers and Fine were subsequently apprehended and spent time in prison. To this day, Leo Burt has escaped capture.

When I graduated high school in the spring of 1972, there was no way Dave and Nancy Glicksman were going to let their son attend Madison. Although my parents were opposed to the war, they didn't pull me out of the rough-and-tumble Peckham Junior High only to go to a college where I would be blown up after 2 am while working in a physics lab. Obviously this was a silly concern because I'd never set foot in a physics lab and the only place I might be after the bars closed at 2 am was a donut shop.

While I partied a lot in Whitewater, it was nothing compared to my first year in Madison. In the fall of 1975, I shared a house at 127 North Hamilton, on the corner of South Hamilton and East Dayton, with eight other guys, all of whom had graduated Whitefish Bay High in 1973, a year after I did. My entry to the house was my friend Melvin Orlove, with whom I had gone to camp and had known for years. Mel and I shared a bedroom in a third-floor attic. There was a broken window in the attic from which we hung a laundry bag full of food. Since the Madison temperatures topped off in the thirties in October and frequently fell well below zero until the end of March, refrigerating cheese and bread from our broken window was a lot easier than racing down two flights of stairs to the kitchen.

Nothing could prepare me for the 1974–75 school year. We had many guests that year who used our house as a makeshift homeless shelter. There was Eugene, a large homeless man in his early 20s who wore a large rumpled overcoat. Eugene would come to our door at 11 pm or midnight, stagger over to our couch with his dog, and pass out. He didn't talk much, but he didn't bother anything, and he left in the morning, so no one wanted to kick him out.

And his dog seemed nice and smelled better than Eugene.

A sketchier guest was the raspy-voiced Antonio, a skinny, five-foot-six street hustler. Sounding like Miles Davis, Antonio had apparently seen the movie *Paper Moon* when it had been released a year earlier in 1973. Or maybe he just coincidentally used the same scam to make a few bucks as Tatum O'Neal had in the film. For those unfamiliar with the scam, an accomplice goes into a store, pays for something with a $20 bill, and leaves. The perpetrator, Antonio in our scenario, goes in and pays for something small with a $5 bill. When the merchant gives him change for the five, Antonio complains that he paid with a twenty. To prove it, he'd say a coed had written her name and phone number on the bill. Sure enough, a $20 bill would be pulled from the register. Lo and behold, the bill had a woman's name and phone number on it, just like Antonio said. Change for the twenty would follow. Of course, to pull this off, an accomplice was needed. On one occasion, he found an assistant in our house.

None of us was above petty crimes to supplement our existence. For a while, I worked at a neighborhood store and turned a blind eye when my roommates came in and left without paying for food or beer. I'd help myself to a few items at the end of my shift as well. We never got in trouble because it turned out the manager was stealing way more from the owner than we were. Apparently, the small items we took were assumed to have been taken by him.

I need to mention my roommate Jim Harrow, perhaps the smartest person at the Hamilton Street house. And that's saying something. Despite nonstop partying, everyone in the house got terrific grades. We were a really smart house. My roommates became engineers, accountants, college professors, and one became a veterinarian. I'd put our cumulative GPA up against any house with eight men in it, other than perhaps the Jewish fraternity.

Like the others, Jim Harrow had grown up in the middle-class Milwaukee suburb of Whitefish Bay. He was a member of one of the two black families that lived in the Bay. Jim was smart, handsome with a killer smile, funny, and on the tennis team.

Other than Mel Orlove, I hadn't known any of my housemates, who were a year behind me in high school. When we lived together in Madison, I enjoyed hanging with a lot of the guys but especially Harrow. He played an acoustic blues guitar and turned me on to Taj Mahal and Yusef Lateef. He played speed chess at the student union and shot pool at Cunique.

Although he was a full-time student, in the two semesters we lived together, I never saw Jim open a textbook until finals week. Then, wired on amphetamines like White Cross and Black Beauties, Jim would tackle a semester's worth of reading for each of his four or five classes in one week. Most of us took speed to study. I certainly did. It helped us stay up late, sometimes even pull an all-nighter. (Interestingly, now when I make it through an entire day without a nap, I call it "pulling an all-dayer.") So while all of us occasionally stayed up and saw the sunrise before a final exam, no one did it like Jim. Night after night, we'd go to bed and Jim would be in our living room studying. We'd get up in the morning and he'd still be there. We'd go to bed the next night, and Jim would still be sitting on the same couch in our living room, studying. I don't have an exact recall of how many nights in a row Jim would stay up, but it had to have been at least three. By the morning of the final exam, Jim looked gray and ashen. But each semester, he earned all Bs and As.

The Hamilton house was incredibly fun. We had a foosball table on one floor. With eight guys living there, there were foosball games going every night. After the ping of each scored goal, someone would yell, "Drink," and we'd all take a pull of our beer. Drugs were abundant. Weed was everywhere. One night, a guy dropped off a tank of laughing gas. Quaalude parties were common.

Things changed for all of us the second semester of the

1974–75 school year. For the first time in decades, bank robberies were taking place in Madison. On Tuesday, January 14, 1975, a bank was robbed. The *Wisconsin State Journal* described the crime this way: "The police hunt continued Tuesday night for a note-passing robber who stuffed $7,450 in his parka pockets and fled about 11 am from the Commercial State Bank at State Street and Capitol Square. 'We've looked at a lot of people, but we have no suspects,' Detective Stanley Davenport told the newspaper."

The fugitive was described as a light-complected black man, age 20 to 25, about five feet, nine inches tall, with moles or freckles on his clean-shaven face, and wearing an army-green hooded parka over a bright-green hooded sweatshirt and black gloves. The bank was located at State Street and Capital Square, just a few blocks from our house. When we looked out the window a few days after the robbery, the top level of the parking garage across the street was lined with police snipers. Their guns were pointed toward our house. Apparently, they were there for Jim Harrow.

Jim's dad, a prominent Milwaukee lawyer, came to Madison, and the matter was cleared up quickly, but it seemed to me that Jim changed after that. School wasn't as important.

During my second and final year in Madison, I lived in the Solveig House. It was a cooperative at 120 W. Gorham Street. Approximately 30 people lived in the house, and in exchange for doing specified chores, each resident paid only $60 a month. There was a treasurer and folks who cleaned or washed dishes. I swept floors and washed dishes. My roommate for the first semester was again Mel Orlove. In my second semester, I shared a room with Mel's girlfriend and later wife, Mim Johnson. It was normal for Mim and me to study, dress, and undress in front of one another. It was also common, though slightly uncomfortable, to listen to Mel and Mim having sex in our room.

During this year, my last in Madison, I got my first car, a 10-year-old Ford Fairlane that my folks had bought for me after I told them I planned to buy a motorcycle. While in college, I always had a job. With my car, I was able to drive to work at my very pleasant job selling men's clothing and shoes at Klitsner's Clothing. One reason it was so pleasant was because Klitsner's also sold women's dancewear. Sid Klitsner's daughter had taken dance lessons as a child, and Sid, unable to find a store that sold leotards, tights, and ballet slippers, began selling dancewear.

It was an absolute pleasure to help women into their ballet slippers ("They should be snug; they stretch out") or toe shoes. I'd have clever lines for the coeds studying dance like "I don't know why they have you ballerinas standing on your toes. Seems like they should just find taller dancers." The best part of the job was women asking my opinion on how they looked when they tried on their Danswear camisoles. I always had a suggestion for a second one they might want to try.

After the 1975–76 school year, I left Madison for law school in Tucson. I rarely went back. But sometime in the 1980s, I returned to Madison with my friend Mike Mahalek, looking for Harrow. We went to Cunique, the student union, and all the places where Jim had hung out years earlier. As we were about to give up and drive out of town, there Jim was, strolling down Gorham Street. We talked and had coffee. After I'd lost touch with Jim in 1975, he'd gone through the motions of student life, and maybe I'm wrong, but I can't help but feel the police singling him out based on race changed his trajectory. Jim had long dread locks. I don't know what else he did after we lived together, but I was glad I found him. He was still smart, funny, and handsome. That day in Madison was the last time I ever saw Jim. After the advent of social media, I tried to find him again but never did. Jim Harrow passed away from cancer in 2016 at age 60.

C H A P T E R 17

Why Did You
Move to Tucson?

Coming to Tucson was the most consequential decision of my life. When I arrived in 1976, I had no idea I'd spend the rest of my life here. So far, anyway. There wasn't a whole lot of culture in Tucson in the mid-1970s, but it sure was beautiful. One tourist attraction claimed to have the Southwest's largest collection of dust.

Until age 21, I'd spent my entire life in Wisconsin. My folks lived in Milwaukee and later in Whitefish Bay. I'd spent summers as a camp counselor in Northern Wisconsin and attended college at Whitewater and then Madison. For reasons I don't fully recall, I was always fascinated with Tucson. Phoenix, Flagstaff, and the rest of Arizona weren't at all appealing. Perhaps as a young kid with asthma, I'd heard that Tucson, with its dry climate, was the place where I'd breathe easier. When I visited a girlfriend in the Old Pueblo in 1975, I knew it was where I'd eventually live.

In the summer of 1974, I'd met Patty, a counselor at a nearby girls' camp. She attended the University of Arizona. We hit it off and spent time together on our days off. In the fall of 1974, while attending the University of Wisconsin-Madison, I hitchhiked 430 miles from Madison to Omaha, Nebraska, over Christmas to meet her family. Hitchhiking in the 1970s was not at all like hitchhiking today. It was safe. On long drives you became friends with the people who stopped to pick you up. Often it was sad when a ride ended because you knew you'd never again see the kind folks who had helped you reach your destination. That same year, Patty came out to visit me in Madison.

Patty and I had a lot in common. We were both Jewish college students who liked to party. If you hadn't noticed from the prior chapters, I took a lot of drugs in the early to mid-70s. In Madison, there was an elderly doctor who would prescribe Quaaludes for any ailment. For a seven-dollar doctor visit and a three-dollar prescription, you could get a month's supply of 30 Quaaludes. Patty was a soulmate. She had a doctor in Tucson who was similarly generous with his prescriptions. I liked Quaaludes.

Paraphrasing Will Rogers, I never met a drug I didn't like. Eventually, I stopped taking Quaaludes. I remember it well. It was when they stopped making them. In 1983, Quaaludes were outlawed because of widespread addiction, recreational abuse, and concerns it was a date-rape drug. This was the drug that Bill Cosby admitted to giving women when he wanted to have sex with them. I didn't know about the addictive qualities or the date-rape stuff. I just knew they were fun to take. I'm not advocating drug use, but during that time, doing drugs was as social as going out with friends for a beer. Everyone did drugs. Even the jocks on the high school football team got stoned.

Partying in college when you had good grades has always been acceptable. If you did well in college and got drunk or stoned all the time, people said, "How great. He's living that college life." If you partied in college and flunked out, those same people said, "Look at that guy. What a loser." Getting good grades let you get away with a lot of stuff that you couldn't otherwise.

Patty and I had a blast together, and in 1975, she invited me to Tucson for my spring break. Because our breaks didn't align, she'd only be able to see me after class in the evenings. She suggested I bring a buddy to hang out with while she was in school. I did. That was the end of my relationship with Patty. She'd come home from class and I'd be nowhere to be found. My friend and I did LSD on our first day in the desert and walked around Sabino Canyon. I immediately fell in love with the Sonoran desert when I looked up at the canyon walls and saw saguaro cacti flipping me the bird. That was the last time I took acid.

The week I was in Tucson, I was rarely at her apartment when Patty finished her classes. I was on Mt. Lemmon, in Nogales, Mexico, or at Reddington Pass. On the few occasions I was home when she finished class, I was usually drunk or stoned. Patty gave me a ride to the airport to return to Madison, and I never saw or spoke to her again. While I'd previously had brief relationships, Patty was my first girlfriend, and I screwed up. All I can say in my defense is that 1) she told me to bring a friend, and I really felt I couldn't just abandon him in Tucson, and 2) I was only 20 years old and did a lot of stupid things. By the end of the trip, two things were clear: Patty was finished with me, and I loved Tucson.

Law school was my way back to Tucson. I applied and was accepted at the University of Arizona College of Law. I arrived here in July 1976. It was over 105 degrees. It was a dry heat. I felt nauseous. I had a dry heave. I watched my shadow evaporate. My worldly belongings were a backpack and a duffel bag as I'd sold my car, a 1965 Ford Fairlane, to pay for my airline ticket. I didn't know anyone in Tucson. Or Arizona.

The first order of business was to secure lodging. After taking a cab from the airport to the law school, I began walking with my backpack and duffel in hand. Without a car, I had to live within walking distance of school. I picked a direction and began walking. I walked south. The heat was oppressive. I saw a dog chasing a rabbit. They were walking. After a half mile lugging around all my worldly possessions and watching my shadow melt, my brain liquified and oozed from of my ears. The soles of my shoes melted and stuck to the pavement. Each step felt like I was pulling my foot out of a newly tarred road. I watched as a funeral procession turned

Me in Tucson around 1981. I got battery acid on my shirt and felt the need to document it for posterity.

into a Dairy Queen drive thru. Since the 1970s nothing has been done to address the ever increasing temperatures. The only idea to lower temperatures in Arizona was to switch from Fahrenheit to Celsius. Arizona has been big on changing to the Metric System. To this day, the only highway in the United States signed in meters instead of miles is Interstate 19 from Tucson to Nogales, Arizona.

I finally found a two-bedroom apartment where I could afford half the rent. After I signed the lease, I asked the landlord how he intended to find my roommate. He politely explained that I had signed the lease, and I was responsible for the entire rent. If I wanted a roommate to share the expense, I'd need to find one. (In hindsight, I should have seen that in the lease, but I hadn't yet started law school.) I put up a notice at the student union and found two roommates.

I decided not to work my first semester of law school. If I flunked out, I didn't want the excuse of having worked. "Yeah, I flunked out, but I had to work and didn't have enough time for my studies." No, if I flunked out, it would be because I had no idea what my professors were talking about.

Although I wouldn't work my first semester, I needed to earn money in the month before classes began. It didn't seem fair for an employer to give me a job in mid-July and then leave in August. That's when I got the idea to donate plasma, as I mentioned earlier. Unlike the sperm bank, the plasma staff didn't make you do the withdrawal yourself, so sitting in a chair and letting them take my blood and then return the plasma-less blood into my arm was easy money. I stopped donating when classes began in August 1976. Forty-six years later, I'm still in Tucson and haven't had to donate plasma ever since.

CHAPTER 18

What Was the Toughest Decision You've Had to Make?

Comedy or law? Law or comedy? At one point, it was a tough decision. I'd always been interested in both. When I had my bar mitzvah in 1967, I was given a box for mementos of the occasion. About 10 years ago, I discovered the box, and among its contents was a *My Bar Mitzvah* book, which asked about my 13-year-old thoughts. It asked about my favorite sports team, teacher, friend, and so on. One question asked was what I thought I'd be when I grew up. I wrote that I wanted to be either a comedian or a lawyer. Turns out I did both. Some would say being a lawyer and a comedian is redundant. Last week, I was introduced at a Rotary event as "the funniest lawyer in Tucson." Obviously, a pretty low bar.

At 13, why did I think I would be a lawyer or a comedian? The answer was television. I didn't know any lawyers. I'd never even met a lawyer. Perhaps law was inevitable; I'm Jewish and can't stand the sight of blood. But the only lawyers I'd ever seen were on television on *Perry Mason* and *The Defenders*. They were smart, clever, and always came up with the right thing to say. They fought against the government, and that appealed to me. There was something heroic and noble about being a criminal defense lawyer and defending the wrongly accused.

My interest in comedy also began with television, specifically *The Dick Van Dyke Show*. My favorite scenes were in the writers' room, watching Robert Petrie, Sally Rogers, and Buddy Sorrell come up with funny sketches and one-liners. Here was a show where people were being paid to be funny. The Baby Boomers, those born between 1946 and 1964, were the first generation to grow up with television as the main entertainment medium. TV shows like *Star Trek* inspired people to be astronauts. *The Dick Van Dyke Show* made me think it was possible to make a living telling jokes.

Although I didn't know any lawyers, I knew lots of funny people. I was genetically predisposed to humor. My mom and my sister Sharon were funny. One family member actually made a living performing. My uncle Oscar Schwartz was a comedy magician similar to, but not as successful as, Carl Ballentine, a brilliant performer in his time. Although my uncle had many careers including military service in World War II, a coin store for serious collectors, and as an appraiser, he always performed comedy/magic. From state fairs to Las Vegas lounge acts or as an opening act for major stars, he did it all. When he died, the Magic Castle in Las Vegas had a "broken wand" ceremony in his honor.

When I was in law school, I didn't realize it, but within a few years I'd face a choice between a career in law or one in comedy. Growing up, I'd always been the class clown or the funny camp counselor. That didn't change in law school. In each class, students were assigned cases to read every night. The next day, professors would cold call a student with questions about the case.

Each night I read the cases and came up with a quip or pun for every case in the event I was called. In some classes, there were up to 60 students. On any given day, the chances I'd be called were remote, but I was always ready. When I had a particularly funny line about a case, I would be disappointed not to be called. When I didn't get the chance to share that quip with the entire class, I whispered it to the lucky few frazzled first-year law students sitting near me who were frantically trying to take notes so they could pass the final exam. First-year law students were a stressed-out bunch in the 1970s. Your two or three hour final exam in each class counted for 100 percent of your final grade. If you knew everything but couldn't recall something or couldn't express it you could fail a class that you had lived and breathed for an entire school year. Things have since changed and today, for the most part, once you're accepted into law school, you're going to graduate.

One day, Professor Ares, a former dean of the law school and clerk to Justice William O. Douglas, called on me about a case. I had my joke ready, told it, and the entire class burst out in sustained laughter. After the laughter died down, Dean Ares looked me in the eye and, in his most stern tone, said, "Mr. Glicksman, there is a time and place for jokes. Being in a law school class or in a courtroom is no place for jokes. Do you understand?" The entire class grew as silent as a falling snowflake. I paused, waited a beat ... two beats ... and then asked, "But, Professor, what if it's really funny?"

My classmates selected me to be the law school graduation speaker for the class of 1979, University of Arizona Law School. I was selected because I was funny, did imitations of our professors, and didn't mind pushing against the boundaries of good taste. However, I was also a very good student. I was in the Order of the Coif, which has nothing to do with having great hair, although I did. The Order of the Coif was awarded to students finishing in the top 10 percent of their law school class. It was a steep climb to get to the top 10 percent after a very slow start in law school with straight Cs my first semester. At that point, I was probably near the bottom of my class. I considered quitting and moving back to Wisconsin, but I stuck around. The next semester, I received all As, and over the last two years, I never had another C.

Prior to the commencement, the current dean and Dean Ares approached me with their concerns about my graduation speech. They warned me, "Although this might be a joke to you, for many of the graduates and their families, this is a very solemn event." I killed. I imitated our tax professor, Arthur Andrews. The keynote speaker was a Ninth-Circuit judge, Thomas Tang. I quipped, "Judge Tang ... isn't that the judge the astronauts took with them to the moon?" (Tang was a powdered orange drink whose advertisements boasted that the astronauts had taken their product into space.) While not a hysterically funny line, from grade school forward, I had learned that poking fun at authority figures at a serious event was an easy laugh.

Along these same lines, I've become something of a roast master over the years, and there are two caveats I learned about roasts or insult comedy: 1) Only punch up. Don't roast or insult folks who aren't successful or prominent. 2) Always end with the schmaltz. That's Yiddish slang for sentimentality. You always want to end with sweet, sentimental praise no matter how you've roasted someone. I ended the graduation speech the way all graduation speeches were supposed to end, reflecting on our years together and looking forward to the vast possibilities that were our future.

In the fall of 1979, I became the class clown who was now going to practice law. I was hired by attorney Bob Hirsh. Bob was a criminal lawyer, although no one could prove it. Kidding aside, Bob was a brilliant criminal defense lawyer. I spent my first year doing Bob's grunt work, researching and writing motions. I wanted to try a case in the worst way, which is exactly what I wound up doing. The first time I went to court, I defended a woman who'd received a parking ticket. Three day trial. My defense was that where she'd parked, the sign said, "Fine for parking."

Now I was going to do what I had always dreamed of as a 13-year-old: defend the wrongly accused and take on the government. It turned out not at all to be the heroic role I envisioned. My clients were almost always guilty, at least of something. Moreover, in the era of mandatory prison sentences, it was unwise to go to trial on most cases even if you had a decent defense. Mandatory prison meant just that. No matter how nice your client was or whether it was a first-time offense, a judge was not allowed to put them on probation even if the judge wanted to.

Here's an example. Possession of $250 worth of cocaine was a mandatory five-year prison sentence. Even in 1979, that was not a large amount of cocaine. An undercover officer would make the buy and make sure that sale was over $250, sometimes even if the seller wanted less money. It would often be a college student or someone selling a small quantity so they could have a small stash for themselves.

You could go to trial and perhaps raise entrapment or move to suppress evidence before trial, but the state would say, "Here's your plea offer. You can avoid prison and have probation available, but you have to take the deal before the judge rules on the pretrial motion." In that case, you couldn't risk going to trial even with a possible defense, knowing that if you lost, your client, a first-time offender, would have to spend five years in prison.

Arizona juries were tough. While selecting a jury in a first-degree murder case, the prosecutor needed to determine potential jurors' views on capital punishment. He asked, "If the defendant were convicted, would you be willing to impose the death penalty?" One elderly woman stood up and answered, "Well, I work during the week, but if you set it on a Saturday I could." The prosecutor held all the leverage, and if you were offered a "probation available" plea in a mandatory time case, you almost always had to accept it.

Being a criminal defense attorney was very difficult. I dealt on an almost daily basis with people who believed they were morally superior to criminal defense attorneys. I heard things like "I could never defend someone who is guilty of (fill in the most despicable crime here)." People associate the attorney with the person they're defending and hate defense attorneys almost as much as the perpetrator.

In 1981, after only two years with Hirsh, I left his office and stopped doing criminal defense work. It was a difficult time. My brief two-year marriage to a fine human who was not interested in ever having a family was ending. I questioned whether I would love anyone else or if anyone would love me. I walked around with a dark cloud over my head. I needed to snap out of it. Comedy clubs or bars doing a comedy night had begun cropping up in Tucson. It's one thing to react to something and have a funny response. It's entirely different to be introduced to an audience as someone who's funny and then go onstage to make them laugh.

Maybe doing comedy would get me out of my funk and force me to look at the humorous side of things. I was a little nervous about doing standup in a bar because after only two years practicing law, I very much wanted to be respected as a lawyer. As a very young lawyer, potential clients already sat across my desk closely scrutinizing me, glancing up at my diploma to see when I'd received it. Efforts to appear more mature and get taken seriously, including growing a beard, would surely be undermined if I were to be on stage telling jokes.

A mutual friend had introduced me to Nick Sievert, a talented, funny man. Nick could play guitar, juggle, sing, dance, and most of all he could Beef Honey. Nick and I decided to be a comedy team, and Bob and Bob was born. Any reluctance to do comedy in bars was grounded in a concern that I could wreck my day job. That's why we were Bob and Bob, not Nick and Elliot. Years later as a solo act, I still worried that judges, opposing lawyers and, worst of all, jurors would not take me seriously as a lawyer. That concern continued in later years when I still wouldn't perform under my true name.

Bob and Bob was a comedy team not because we had routines that required a duo or because one of us was a natural straight man to the other. We were a comedy team because we were both scared to try standup comedy alone.

We decided we'd perform together. On Sunday evenings, we worked in my townhouse located in the Riverview Townhouses, writing and rehearsing bits but never performing them for one month, two months, six months. "We're not ready yet." "This could be funnier." "We should say this word at the end of the sentence, not in the middle, to punch the joke." We were terrific at making excuses but terrible at performing comedy. We were excusing our way out of ever seeing if we were funny. You really can't know if comedy works until you perform it for an audience. A musician can listen to a recording of his music and know if it's good. With comedy, something can look good on paper, or sound good when you rehearse it, but until you do it for an audience, you really don't know if your material is funny. We were just scared to perform and watch the audience squirm in their seats and hear their uncomfortable pity laughs.

In November 1981, Bob and Bob made their debut at Tequila Mockingbird, a local bar and restaurant, because we had no choice. The week leading up to the open mic night, Nick and I told everyone we knew that we were going to perform our brand-spanking-new comedy show. Once we did that and our friends began telling us they'd be there, there was no way out.

Comedy isn't comedy until it's performed. Until then, it's just some stuff you think is funny. Schrodinger's cat is simultaneously dead and alive in its box until someone observes it. A tree doesn't make a sound in the forest unless someone hears it. You can't know if what you've written is funny until an audience hears it.

Nick and I paced the Tequila Mockingbird parking lot, going over every line. "Pause there. Take a beat." "Say it this way." We smoked a joint. We paced some more. We went inside. Oh, great. There was another comedy team going on, Gomez and Gomez! You've got to be kidding me. I was sure neither was named Gomez. And they were dressed funny. One Gomez had giant pointed shoes like an elf, and the other was wearing a fishing-net type shirt with bottle caps and assorted flair hanging from it. Pointed-shoe Gomez started the act with his imitation of a moth and repeatedly bashed his forehead into a light bulb he was holding. People began laughing.

That's when fate smiled on the team of Bob and Bob. On the fourth time whacking the light bulb against his forehead, the bulb shattered into shards of glass. Elf-shoe Gomez had a gash on his forehead, and blood appeared. A rivulet of blood began to run down his face, along the inner side of his eye, and down his nose. The audience was horrified. Gomez and Gomez made a hasty exit from the stage, with bloody Gomez grabbing a cocktail napkin off a table to staunch the bleeding. Happy days. As long as we didn't projectile vomit on the front row of tables, Bob and Bob were sure to get a better response than bloody elf-shoed Gomez. And we did. But our positive audience response was not because we were particularly funny; it was because it was 'our' crowd ... We had papered the crowd with an audience that would have belly laughed and knee slapped if we had just stood there making fart sounds with our armpits. It wasn't a true test, but we were encouraged.

Some bits seemed to generate real laughs. The confessional bit about a horny priest enjoying confessional more than he should from Billy, a penitent teenager reluctant to tell his priest about the urges he struggled with when seated behind Mary Jo McConnoll in biology class; a judgmental talking bank machine questioning a customer about his purchases; and bits about dating were legitimately funny.

Most bits were funny, slightly dirty, and juvenile, but the oldest Jewish astronaut, Buster Nosecohen, was truly awful. I think we were channeling Mel Brooks's/Carl Reiner's two-thousand-year-old man. We never did it again. Fortunately, cell phones didn't exist, so there are no videos of that routine. All in all, it went okay. No blood had been spilled during our performance, and folks had laughed, but to measure whether we were funny, we needed to perform in front of people other than our friends.

And we did: writing and rehearsing every Sunday and performing every Tuesday at Tequila Mockingbird. After several solid weeks, we were asked to host the Tuesday night shows.

Bob and Bob in 1982

In 1981, around the same time I began doing comedy, I became partners with an elderly lawyer, Will Essig. I saw him, and still see him, as "elderly" even though I'm older now than he was when I began working with him. Will really was elderly; having survived heart attacks and cancer, he was frail. I put a semi colon in the previous sentence not just because it's grammatically correct, but coincidentally because I think Will also had part of his colon removed. He had a broad civil practice, which he had begun before the era of specialization. Will was an old-school lawyer, the family lawyer who would do Uncle Joe's drunk driving charge, sister Sally's divorce, son George's bankruptcy, and the occasional personal injury case. In fact, there was no legal case he wouldn't take. I once told him, "Will, we can't take an eminent domain case. We're not experts in eminent domain law." His response was, "Expert, schmexpert. You read the case law, and then you're an expert."

In 1982, Bob and Bob opened for Ricky Nelson, and a

reviewer wrote that we "unleashed some funny topical material" that was "very, very funny." That same year, we bombed as a last-minute replacement for the opening act for the Little River Band. The audience was expecting a musician who, at the time, had a Top 40 hit. The way I remember it, the announcement went something like this: "Ladies and gentlemen, John Stewart can't be here this evening." Boo. Booo! Booooo! "Instead, here's Bob and Bob." BOOOOOO!!!

At the end of 1982, when we performed with a comedy duo at the local Invisible Theatre, a reviewer from the now-defunct *Tucson Citizen* wrote that Bob and Bob "tell jokes from a wryly suburban point of view" and enjoyed a bit where the Super Bowl was replaced with Vietnam veterans playing in the Agent Orange Bowl and cheerleaders in Viet Conga lines.

Will Essig died in July 1983. I began dating Lorraine in May 1983. After Will's death, I learned that he hadn't paid withholding taxes on my salary and that he'd committed the serious ethical violation of having commingled the office trust account with our operating account. A trust account contains money belonging to clients and not the lawyers. The money is held in trust until it is earned by the attorney.

To make matters worse, Essig's widow (Betty) insisted that the $100,000 that Will and I had set aside to pay her upon his death was insufficient and threatened to sue me. When he died, Will was in the process of drafting a written agreement indicating what Betty would receive upon his death, but he died before the agreement was reduced to writing. I was 29 years old, had no idea how to run a law office, and was facing financial ruin. I hired a Big Eight accounting firm to straighten out my books and negotiate an IRS settlement. (And yes, I had to go to trial in Cochise County, Arizona, on that eminent domain case. I read the cases and became an expert.) A lawyer friend assisted me and convinced Will's widow's lawyer that she ought to be grateful for the $100,000 that had been set aside for her. In the four months following my law partner's death, I didn't see Lorraine.

Lorraine and I began seeing each other again in the fall of 1983. I spent the first night at her house on October 3, 1983. I know the date because that was the day my townhouse was flooded, and three nearby units fell into the Rillito River as floodwaters undercut the banks beneath the buildings. Firefighters evacuated the remaining townhouses, and I spent the night at Lorraine's. We began living together in the summer of 1984.

October 3, 1983, photo of the Riverview Townhouses, where I lived. My unit was the second from the end at the far right. Three units on the left side of the photo fell into the river when the water undercut the banks supporting the structures. The Rillito was usually a dry riverbed during this time, but days of rains converted it into a river. My complex changed its name from Riverview to Pima Park Townhouses after the floods. My evacuation gave me the opportunity to spend my first night at Lorraine's house. (Photo - Emmet Jordan/Arizona Daily Star)

By the end of 1984, Bob and Bob had gone as far as we could in Tucson. My talented friend Nick moved to Seattle to do some theater. He lived with his sister and her husband there. "Elliot, you should come up. There's a great comedy scene up here. It's a big city. I think Bob and Bob could work." Decision time arrived. I was single. My law practice was solid, if not spectacular. I was going to trial on difficult civil cases and, more often than not, winning. The IRS withholding tax and the trust account issues had been resolved. I had a new law partner, Don Awerkamp, who, although over a dozen years older than me, had started practicing law a couple years after I did. Don had been a priest before going to law school, and in contrast to most attorneys, he practiced patience and kindness while becoming a very effective lawyer.

If I was going to do comedy, this was my time. I was 29 years old. I had sold my townhouse, so I wasn't tied down with a mortgage. (After the October 1983 flood, it was sold at a loss ... go figure.) I wanted to give comedy a try. What about my law practice that was finally taking off? Walking in Sabino Canyon in Tucson has always been a great way to sort out my thoughts. After going out to the desert with my friend Tony and ingesting psilocybin, I made a decision. I had clarity. I'd go to Seattle for a month, do some showcases with Nick, and see how it felt.

Still mildly tripping, I went to Don Awerkamp's house and told him my plan. "I'm going to Seattle to do comedy for a month. If I like it and think it'll work, you can have the law practice ... furnishings, copy machine, office equipment, and all of our cases. You won't owe me a thing. If it doesn't work, I'll come back and throw myself into the practice of law. Deal?" Don agreed. That day in early February 1985 was the last time I ever did any hallucinogenics.

But what about Lorraine? I was in love with her and wanted to start a family. Lorraine was 33 with an 11-year-old daughter. There was no way she'd leave Tucson. If I came back, would she still be waiting for me? What would she think? I told her. She understood. If I didn't try, I'd regret it.

In March 1985, I drove my Toyota Corolla to Seattle to do standup for a month with Nick. I arranged for a local florist to deliver a rose to Lorraine every day at the law office where she worked. A line of poetry would be included with each day's delivery. In the event I chose law, I was going to do everything I could from my end to be sure Lorraine was still there when I returned to Tucson in April.

Being on stage in Seattle was great ... for the three to five minutes we performed. The other 23 hours and 55 minutes were not as great. I'd be up till one or two in the morning, wired from the brief set we'd done. I'd smell like cigarette smoke because in 1985, smoking was still allowed everywhere. (Some places had carved out small areas for smokers, but that was like having a part of the pool where people could pee.) After only a couple of weeks, I'd made my decision. I'd return to Tucson, practice law, continue to do comedy as a hobby, marry Lorraine, have kids, and live happily ever after. And that's exactly what I did. The decision wasn't difficult, especially with Lorraine there in Tucson.

You may ask, "But what happened to Bob and Bob? Did Nick stay in Seattle and find a new comedy partner?" You'll have to read the next chapter for the answer.

CHAPTER 19

What Happened to Bob and Bob?

After doing comedy with my buddy Nick in March 1985, I returned to Tucson to marry Lorraine and to practice law. I'd decided that comedy would be a hobby. I was still concerned that if I did standup in bars, I wouldn't be taken seriously as an attorney, so I needed a stage name for my solo act. My name changed pretty much from one show to the next. One night, I'd go up as Dirk Winston, another as Nunzio Spumoni. If I was doing two sets at a club and the first show bombed, I'd change my name for the second show. One night, the emcee asked me my name. I told him that he could introduce me with any name he liked. When it was my turn to perform, he said, "Ladies and gentlemen, please welcome Danny Boskowitz."

I liked the name. It was an old-school sort of Borscht Belt-sounding name. Years later, with my reputation as a competent lawyer secure, I began using my real name onstage. I told folks that I decided to use Elliot Glicksman because Danny Boskowitz sounded too Jewish.

I was a local comedy success. Working clean and having a solid 25 minutes, I was tabbed to be the opening act for Gilbert Gottfried, Phyllis Diller, and Jerry Seinfeld. I frequently middled at Laffs, a local comedy club.

Lorraine and me after opening for Jerry Seinfeld for a couple of shows. Hope things turned out okay for the guy. He seemed nice.

Had the pleasure of doing four shows over two nights with Phyllis Diller. She was **75** years old at the time and was hysterical.

In many ways, doing a solo act was easier than being part of team. First, clubs pay performers by the act, not by the number of people in the act. If you were a duo, you each got half. Second, to be funny as a team, you had to both be "on" for the bit to work. If one of you was "off," the bit wouldn't work. Finally, a team needs to agree on what to do. In the beginning for Nick and me, it was easy. We wrote stuff and performed it. Over time, I became more obsessed with each word in the bit. I would take out unnecessary words or replace a single word with one that was funnier than the word we'd been using. We disagreed on which bits to do. One night I told Nick I wanted to do our dating bit. He didn't want to do it. I really wanted to do it. He didn't. I said the first line of the bit. Nick stood silently. I walked off the stage. More than once, one of us would get mad at the other and storm off the stage or, even worse, get mad onstage.

We'd had disagreements when we did comedy for a month in Seattle. When I returned to Tucson to marry

A poster from a rare Bob and Bob reunion with our friends David Fitzsimmons and Nancy Stanley in 2016

Lorraine and commit to practicing law, Nick stayed in Seattle. Eventually, he returned to Tucson and had a successful career writing, directing, and performing in local theater. But Nick never did solo standup. Over the years, we both became members of various comedy groups: the Sweatlodge, a sketch comedy/standup comedy group that performed in the mid-1990s, and the Arroyo Cafe Players, a large ensemble assembled by our mutual friend Dave Fitzsimmons that does a Christmas show every year in Tucson. On very rare occasions, in the Sweatlodge, the Arroyo Cafe Players, and other venues, Bob and Bob will reunite, to the delight of my son Ben.

Here are four routines we used to do: dating, baseball announcer, granfalloon, and cheeses. Hope they're funny on paper.

DATING
E: After being married this long, there's a little piece of me that envies you.
N: And I bet I know what little piece that is.
E: Must be quite the life. Do whatever you want.
N: Do whatever I want!
E: Don't compromise for anybody.
N: Don't compromise for anybody!
E: Date lots of women.
N: Don't compromise for anybody!
E: Wait, you're kidding. You don't have a lot of dates?
N: Even my hand's sick of me.
E: Well, let's figure out the problem. Let's role play.
N: Role play. Great. You be an onion roll, and I'll be a kaiser.
E: No, role play. I'll be you, and you be on a date with you.
N: You're gonna be me, and I'm gonna be on a date with me?
E: Exactly! You start.
N: It's been a lovely evening. My boyfriend is waiting for me out in the car.
E: No, no, no. This is the *beginning* of the date.

N: Oh. The beginning of the date.

E: Why, sure. Now you start.

N: It's been a lovely evening. My boyfriend is waiting for me out in the car.

E: No. Look ... she's interested in you.

N: Oh. Oh. She's interested in me.

E: Yes. She's interested in you. So now you start.

N: Do you have any money?

E: No!

N: Do you drive a Ferrari?

E: No!

N: It's been a lovely evening. My boyfriend is waiting for me out in the car.

E: Stop it. Listen. I'm gonna help you. Let me walk you through a date.

N: You're going to walk me through it?

E: Yes. Okay. It's your first date You go up to her door, and you want to break the ice, so you say ... ?

N: Don't be afraid of me?

E: No!

N: Be afraid of me. Be very, very afraid of me. Grrrr.

E: Stop with the afraid of me. You take her out to dinner. Someplace like ... ?

N: McDonald's?

E: Nicer.

N: Chipotle?

E: No place with a drive-thru. We'll work on it. You have a couple of cocktails and say, "Are you ... ?"

N: Drunk yet?

E: "Having a good time." And later you take her home and look into her eyes and say, "Tonight has been very ... ?"

N: Expensive?

E: Special! And you go into your place and put on some classical music.

N: Megadeath?

E: Maybe some Mozart, Bach, or Shubert.

N: No Shubert.

E: No?

N: We had ice cream at the restaurant.

E: And you dim the lights and light a couple of . . . ?

N: Joints?

E: Candles. And then you break out . . . ?

N: In a rash?

E: A bottle of . . . ?

N: Calamine lotion?

E: Calamine lotion?

N: For the rash!

E: Wine!

N: (whining) For the rash!

E: (with N closely following and repeating the phrase) You break out a bottle of wine!

N: And what does she do then? What does she say?

E: She says, "It's been a lovely evening. My boyfriend is waiting for me in the car."

GRANFALLOON

E: It's actually nice to be riding the subway in New York again.

N: You must not be from here. No one from New York talks to anyone on the subway.

E: No. From a small Wisconsin town.

N: No kidding? Me too. Really small town. Cedarberg.

E: Cedarberg? No way. I'm from Cedarberg. Cedarberg High?

N: Only high school in Cedarberg! Class of '72.

E: Class of '72? Me too. Amazing. Only 75 kids in our graduating class and to run into one in New York. Wow!

N: Great memories of high school. Especially a small school like that. The closeness.

E: Yeah ... sometimes too close. Everyone knew everyone and knew everybody's business.

N: Yeah. A fishbowl sometimes. But wouldn't trade it.

E: No, I wouldn't trade our little class for anything.

N: Yeah. Wow. Bob Girth.

E: Hi, Bob. I'm Bob Trout. Nice to meet you.

N: Can't say I can place you though. (pause) But we all change, right?

E: Not sure I remember you either. Remember John Blake?

N: John Blake?

E: Class president. Quarterback of the football team. Walked with a limp.

N: Huh. Seems like I should remember him.

E: Glass eye. He'd have different ones. Had a bloodshot one. At parties he'd pop one out, and say 'I'll keep an eye out for you.'

N: Cedarberg High?

E: Cedarberg, Wisconsin. Yep. Yep. Class of '72.

N: Well, I know who you'll remember. The Malatch sisters.

E: Who?

N: The Malatch sisters. The twins.

E: Twins? Boy, not ringing a bell.

N: Conjoined. They were conjoined twins. (E shaking his head no.) At the top of their heads. They'd stand as far apart as they could, and we'd do a limbo line. Limbo under the Malatch arch there.

E and N: Cedarberg. Cedarberg High!

E: One thing I know you'll remember. Meanest teacher in the school.

N: Remember her? Heck, I had her for math!

E: Her?

N: Yeah, old lady Dunn.

E: Who?

N: Old lady Dunn.

E: No.

N: Hunchback.

E: Nuh-uh.

N: Had a fake arm. Sometimes it fell out of her sleeve.

E: Hey. It's been a long time.

N: At least we'll always share the memories of our
winning team.

E: State champions!

N: (excited) That's right. State champions in basketball!

E: Basketball? Football. State champs in football. All hail
the Cedarberg Pigeons.

N: Pigeons? The Blue Dukes.

E and N each begin singing different school fight songs.

E: Well, hey, this is my stop.

N: Well, that was awesome. Thanks, man.

E: Great memories.

N: Yeah. See ya.

E exits.

N: Pigeons?

CHEESES

E: (southern preacher accent) Can I help you, sir?

N: Yeah, the name drew me in. Born Again Cheese Store.
What is that, cheese to milk and back to cheese again?

E: No, it's—

N: I got it. Is it cheese from Reincarnation milk?

E: No, my son. You see, I've devoted my life to serving
cheeses.

N: I gotta go. I think my bus is here.

E: Ah, my son. Years ago, I was like you. I was lost. I was
wandering through the forest, and what did I see?

N: What did you see?

E: A little log church. It was the cottage cheeses. Do you
know what happened next?

N: I cheddar to think about it.

E: I went home that night looking for a sign. I put a
souffle in the oven, and what did I see?

N: What did you see?

E: The cheeses had risen.

N: And it was gouda!

E: Son, are you ready to accept cheeses into your

heartburn?

N: I am. Give me cheeses!

E: Then you are ready to accept cheeses for your own personal salivation?

N: Yes, I'm salivating already.

E: This one is from a small town in Israel.

N: Could it be . . . ?

E: Cheeses of Nazareth!

N: Praise cheeses. Give me cheeses.

E: This one right heah ... I say this one right heah is a dehydrated mozzarella. I say a dehydrated mozzarella. It's not only good for you complexion; it's great for your soul.

N: You mean?

E: Yes. Cheeses dried for our skins. Sing with me.

Together: Block of aged cheddar cheese

 Most religious are the bries

 From our faith, eternal bliss

 Father, son, and holey Swiss

 Block of aged cheddar cheese

 Most religious are the bries

THE BASEBALL ANNOUNCER

E: Brian Jones here for the start of a new season of Wildcat baseball. And I'd like to welcome our new color man. Here to analyze all the action is former Major Leaguer Zippy Pullay. Welcome aboard, Zippy!

N: Thanks, Brian. Great to be here. One teensy correction. Never actually made it to the Majors. Didn't make the Bigs. But again, looking forward to callin' all the action with you today.

E: Oh, sorry. Well, a lot of very talented ballplayers don't make it to the show. Takes a lot of talent but also takes a lot of luck too.

N: You got that right. After I finished my rehab stint, I was never the same. That was rough.

E: I'm sure it was. Rehab for a blown-out knee, Tommy John surgery?

N: Funny story. It was pain pills, Brian. And the booze. Coke, too, if I'm gonna be completely honest. And it was six stints in rehab to really—

E: Okay, Zippy. Well, you don't have to have played in the bigs to analyze a game. Minor League Baseball, seeing folks on the way up and on the way down, is really the heart and soul of this great pastime.

N: Well, actually, Brian ...

E: You played Minor League Baseball, right?

N: Actually, funny story, Brian. See, when I was nine years old, I was five-foot, three inches. So you'd think I was gonna really be a big guy. The trajectory was looking good, right?

E: And?

N: Yeah, then it just stopped. Never grew any more.

E: Never?

N: Not an inch. Half an inch. But not an inch.

E: College ball? Intramural? High school?

N: Funny thing about that too, Brian. See, the other kids just kept growing. By ninth grade they were a lot bigger than me. Stronger too.

E: But you were faster, right? Zippy. Your name is Zippy. You must have zipped around those bases.

N: You'd think so, but actually, in addition to the growth spurt that never came, my legs are disproportionately short compared to the rest of me ... sort of like a human Pomeranian. You've seen those dogs.

E: But your name's Zippy.

N: Yeah. Funny—

E: Story about that too. Right. I get it.

N: Yeah. So funny story there, Brian. When I was a senior in high school, some of the bigger kids pulled my pants down. Depantsed me, I think you call it, and stuffed me in a locker.

E: Rough kids, huh?

N: Oh, yeah. Probably would've been worse if it were the boys. So anyway, you really can't pull up your pants when you're in a locker.

E: No, I'd guess not.

N: It's a real snug fit in there. So a couple days later when someone opened the door, I pulled up my pants, and the zipper—

E: Yeah, I get it.

N: Got stuck ... and not on any fabric.

E: I think it's time for the first pitch.

N: And I've been Zippy ever since. Zippy Pullay. Okay, let's play ball!

We had other routines, but these four are a pretty good representation. If you enjoyed these, find a video of Bob and Ray doing the "Slow Talkers of America." Those guys were an inspiration.

CHAPTER 20

Did you keep a journal after your granddaughter Mackenzie was born?

Why yes, I did keep a journal after Mackenzie was born. On the evening of February 8, 2022, Lorraine and I arrived at the neonatal intensive care unit of an Idaho Falls hospital just a few hours after Mackenzie was born. The next day, Zach tried, with limited success, to get his daughter to take a bottle. "Better start suckin', sistah, or you'll never get out of here!" These were funny words of encouragement from our son Zach to his daughter, but these words are only appropriate in a neonatal intensive care unit, as opposed to, for example, a dungeon.

I never kept journals or diaries, but I memorialized the first month of my granddaughter Mackenzie's life. She is nearly five months old and still hasn't read it. Makes me wonder why I bothered to write it.

She really hasn't done much of anything. The kid's getting by on her good looks which, I have explained to her, will fade. Visiting her folks last night, Zach asked if I'd put her down. "You're nothing but a huge burden on your parents," I told her looking into her wide toothless smile. If Zach wanted me to put Mackenzie to bed, he should have said so.

Zach and Robin selected *Mackenzie*, a traditional Jewish name. Moses tripped on his robe coming down from Sinai, and cried, "Dammit! Why didn't I wear my kilt". Mackenzie need not be a Scot. She can be Scott-*ish*. My wife Lorraine was raised Catholic. But after all these decades with me, she's become Jew-*ish*. Someday when I take Mackenzie to a deli, it'll likely be a corned beef on rye for me and haggis with a shmear of horseradish for her.

Here's my journal of her first month.

2.22.22 A Twosday in Twoson

Mackenzie Jane. What a beautiful name. And you're the most beautiful girl in the whole world. Incredibly, you're my granddaughter. What an awesome coincidence! You were born on February 8, your Aunt Jill's birthday. Babies are usually born when a mom is pregnant for 40 weeks, but you arrived when the gestational carrier was just over 33 weeks pregnant. Your grandma Lorraine and I got to see you when you were only eight hours old. You sure know how to make an appearance. I'm guessing this won't be your last incredible entrance. You were little so they had you bundled up in a Plexiglas box, like the display case for my signed Bart Starr helmet. I got to reach my hands in and place them on your chest through an opening on the side. I felt your tiny heart beating, and you were without a doubt the most beautiful thing I'd ever seen in a plexiglass box. Sorry, Bart.

I've been meaning to write down what I remembered about that day and the days that followed but I've been busy getting ready for your arrival in Tucson. Your folks, your Grandparents Mike and Jody, and Lorraine and I were in Los Angeles at your baby shower on Sunday, February 6, when we learned that Jordyn, the woman who carried you in her tummy, was getting ready to give birth. Your mom and dad got on a plane that night and flew to Idaho Falls to await your entry into the world. Your mom and dad weren't able to get the car seat, diaper bag, stroller and all the other things they needed in Tucson to bring you back from Idaho Falls. That same Sunday night, Lorraine and I flew back to Tucson, gathered their stuff and on Tuesday the 8th, we drove to Phoenix with all of your parents' stuff and flew to Idaho.

I keep saying *Lorraine and I* because I'm not sure how you're going to refer to us. Folks have asked us "Are you going to be grandma and grandpa? Will you be Tata and Nana? Abuelo and Abuela?" Honestly, we haven't given a lot of thought to what you should call us. I'm guessing it'll probably be Grandma and Grandpa. That's sort of a default title that people use. But who knows? Maybe you'll decide what to call me. Honestly, I don't care if you call me Boo Boo Von Poopy Face.

Frankly, we're still figuring out what to call you. *Mackenzie Jane* lends itself to all sorts of nicknames. Kenzie, MJ, or Little Z (this one's popular because we call your dad "Z" but we also call him "Zachy Boy"). I guess we could call you Z girl. You could also be called Mac. Lorraine isn't fond of that one. Who knows? Maybe you'll be the one called Boo Boo Von Poopy Face.

The woman that carried you in her tummy was a really kind woman named Jordyn. When Jordyn called your mom and dad on Sunday, February 6, they flew immediately to Idaho so they'd be there when you were born. Sunday turned to Monday and you still weren't born. The doctors said they were going to induce you to come out. I don't know how someone induces a baby to leave the womb but I hoped the doctor could be persuasive. She couldn't offer you a cookie. You didn't have any teeth. So I don't know what they did, but sure enough you were born the next day, Tuesday the 8th.

We hung out in Idaho Falls until Sunday, February 13 and then came back to Tucson. Between your birthday when we arrived and our trip home, we got to see you every day. We got to feed you a bottle. I sang a couple songs to you. I'm not a very good singer but I like singing to you. I like to sing when other people aren't around. Everyone seems to prefer my singing that way. You'll probably have to hear me singing for a while until you are able to talk and say "please, stop singing!"

It was really exciting for Lorraine and I to receive pictures every day from your parents. They also told us how you were progressing in the NICU. NICU was the place you were kept til you got a little bigger and stronger and could go home. To leave the NICU you had to be able to breathe on your own and drink a bottle and stay warm. Your mom and dad would tell us stuff like this from Saturday, February 19, "Through the 24 hour period yesterday (5 am to 5 am) she drank 65% of her bottle. Need her to be >80%. At 7:30 today she took 80% so we'll see if we can keep that trend going." When you get bigger, we'll play Peek A Boo I See You which will be a lot more fun than Nic ICU.

It's so cool that you're here. I'm very excited to get to get to know you. I have a lot of sunrises behind me, and some still ahead of me. You have a huge number of sunrises ahead of you. For a while, we'll both share the same sunrises. I like that. I like that our sunrises overlap now. I can't wait to watch you grow up. You arrive in Tucson on Thursday and lots of people are excited to see you. I'll write more later but bye for now. Boo Boo Von Poopy Face (or Grandpa)

February 26, 2022

Well, it's been a couple days since you arrived back in Tucson on Thursday evening, the 24th. You had your first flight from Idaho Falls to Phoenix and then finally back in Tucson. Apparently you were pretty mellow on the flight. The days leading up to your arrival were busy for us in Tucson. Your Grandma and I took your folks' dog Ollie to be groomed. We did our best to prepare him for your appearance, explaining that he'd have a fur-less little being in his house. We also did some grocery shopping so your parents wouldn't arrive to an empty refrigerator. There has been quite a buzz among all the family members since your birth. You're sort of a big deal. One of the great

ironies of life is that none of us will ever forget these days with you and you will never remember them.

Fortunately, your mom has created a photographic record of every moment of your young life. I'm pretty sure you're currently the most photographed person in the world, including the Royal Family. Seriously, you have only been here 18 days and your mom's album contains 314 pictures and 40 videos. You do the math. Wait you can't. You're a baby. Fine. I'll do it. It's approximately 20 entries a day. And those are only the ones she put in a shared album.

You landed at the Tucson Airport at 10:30 on Thursday. Your mom came down the escalator to the baggage section of the airport holding you. Your dad understandably lagged behind since he was carrying your diaper bag, a backpack and a stroller that had been checked at the gate when they boarded the plane.

Although we had just seen you on the 13th, you had already changed. When we left, you didn't open your eyes very often. Now your eyes were open and you seemed to be checking out your surroundings. Had I known you were going to be that focused, I would have shaved. Babies change a lot. And your mom and dad have changed you a lot. You have some stinky poops. No offense. But I'm trying to give an honest account here like James Boswell. (Look it up.) I expect my every word will likely be very meaningful when future generations are curious about the early days of the woman that cured cancer, brought peace to the world and was a supermodel. I need to be accurate.

I got to hold you. Twice. You are so beautiful. In a world where people have attention spans that last only for a 30-second soundbite or the length of a 45-second Tik Tok video, I can just hold you and stare at your little hands and feet and your beautiful face for hours.

Your Uncle Ben, Aunt Kelsey and Auntie Jill all flew to Tucson to see you. Jill had planned to come this weekend because every year she and your dad usually go to a music festival in Tempe together. Obviously, they aren't going. Your dad has hardly complained at all that he won't see the *Foo Fighters* or *Black Puma.*

Ben and Kelsey and Jill loved taking turns holding you. My earlier statement that you're the most beautiful girl in the whole world is not an opinion. It is an objective fact. Jill, Ben, Kelsey, Robin's mom and sister all agree. Lest you think, it's only family members, you should know that everyone I approach with a picture and ask, "Don't you think this is the most beautiful girl in the whole world?" answers "Yes". Every single person. Well, except for this one guy. Showing him Mackenzie's picture and asking, "Don't you think she's the most beautiful girl in the world?", this jerk just stared and asked me if I wanted "fries with that". Guessing that McDonalds serves Unhappy Meals.

Zach was talking to us about your doctor visit yesterday when he mistakenly said he'd taken you to the vet, instead of the pediatrician. At least I think he was mistaken when he said it. It'd be weird if at your first doctor visit, the doc just felt your nose to see if it was wet and said you didn't have fleas. Zach saying "vet" instead of "pediatrician" is an honest mistake. Your dad had a great dog named Gracie who died six months ago. Your dad and Gracie had a great life together, even before your dad met your mom. I'm sure you'll see pictures of Gracie. She was a very good girl.

Your folks seem to really have taken to this whole parenting thing. They love you so much. It's really cool to see.

March 9, 2022

Yesterday was your one month birthday. Wow time flies. Seems like only a few weeks ago, you were only a week old. Your grandma (which is what I guess I'll call her) went over to your house yesterday. She fed you and I held you. Your dad thought you needed a diaper change. He was right. But when he took off your diaper, you weren't finished yet. You looked like a baby soft serve chocolate ice cream machine. He kept wiping and you kept serving. He had a hard time keeping up. It was like Lucy in the candy factory. That's a reference you might not get. It's a reference your dad might not get (and your mom definitely won't understand). It's an old reference to a TV show when I was a baby. You can look it up on You Tube if that is still a thing when you read this. I say your mom won't understand the reference to Lucy, not to be insulting. I love your mom, but she doesn't get a lot of the cultural references I use. Your dad gets these old references because we exposed him to a lot of the old television shows, movies and music that your grandma and I enjoyed when we were young. I think your dad is a little embarrassed because he can recognize songs by Dean Martin, Miles Davis and Barry Manilow.

Years ago, your dad asked your mom if she could name all four Beatles. Your mom thought they were John, George, Ringo and Paul Simon. She was so close. There was a Paul in the Beatles, but his name was Paul McCartney. Paul Simon was a member of another great group in the sixties. Simon & Garfunkel. Gosh, there's so much music history you need to learn. There's a lot more history for you to learn than when I was a kid. A lot has happened since your grandma and I were little. Hopefully, we'll be around to tell you some of the stuff we got to see like the moon landing, or when President Kennedy was killed. Your grandma was at the funeral procession for President Kennedy in Washington DC. Well, I rambled a bit here. All I really wanted to say was how fun it was seeing you on your one-month birthday.

CHAPTER 21

Did You Document Your Granddaughter's Birth?

My answer to this isn't all that humorous. If you've read everything up to this point, it may not be all that different from the previous chapters. Our son Zach and his wife, Robin, became parents, via surrogacy, to Mackenzie Jane Glicksman. Those first dramatic weeks — gestational carrier water breaks six and a half weeks prematurely, induced labor and mystical birth — are documented. Now the child rearing begins.

Before I give some thoughts on raising a child, does anyone really use the phrase *child rearing*, as in *child-rearing techniques*? Or *I reared my child*? Don't answer. I'd rather not know. For what it's worth, here are some thoughts on raising a child.

1. United you stand, divided you fall. You and your partner need to be a united front when raising your child. If not, your kid will quickly learn that they can go to Mom or Dad to get what they want. Given the times, I should say they'll learn to go to Mom or Dad or other Mom or other Dad. Let's just say *parents*. If parents disagree on issues like discipline, bedtime, or whether a nine-year-old is too young for a Stephen King movie, work those issues out privately. This technique, known as "Do what your mother said," provides a united front for your kid.

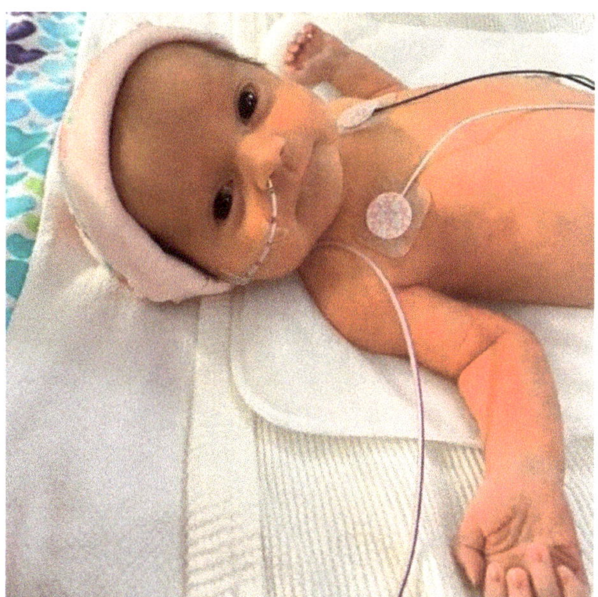

Mackenzie Jane Glicksman, the most beautiful girl in the whole world

2. Don't fight in front of your child. You are your child's world, their universe. If you have a disagreement or argue, do it privately. Nothing terrifies a kid more than the idea that Mommy and Daddy are fighting. Ok, letting a nine-year old watch a Stephen King movie might scare them too. Not that I have any reason to know that. Really. Completely guessing on that one. But yeah probably would be real scary.

3. Rituals make memories. Any ritual, no matter how small or silly, will become a special memory for your son or daughter. If you make pancakes every Sunday, decorate them and boldly announce, "It's Pancake Sunday!" I guarantee that Sundays will forever be remembered as Pancake Sunday. When our kids were little, instead of gently tucking them in at night, we'd bounce them up and down on their mattress and tell them it was a *bumpy snuggle*. Ben and Zach are both in their 30s and fondly remember bumpy snuggles despite the silly name. I could be wrong here, and they would never admit it, but I'm guessing they'd enjoy a bumpy snuggle from their mom and me even now.

4. Compromise with the other parent. Lorraine really didn't want our boys to pitch or catch when they played Little League Baseball. She was concerned they'd be smacked with a hard-hit line drive off of an aluminum bat. She also insisted that they wear a face mask on their batting helmets. Zach was a good pitcher. He wanted to pitch, and he did pitch in a few games. When Zach went to the mound, Lorraine went to the car. Clearly, it was more important to Lorraine that Zach not pitch than it was to either Zach or me that he did. Despite baseball fans everywhere being deprived of the opportunity to see Zach Glicksman break Nolan Ryan's record for throwing the most no-hitters, it gave Lorraine peace of mind and got her out of the car. By the way, Lorraine's unfounded concerns existed even before Ben's nose was broken by a thrown baseball.

Raising children in the Jewish faith was really important to me and not as important to Lorraine. Additionally, her maternal grandmother had been Jewish but converted to marry Ray O'Day. Lorraine went along with my strong desire to raise Jewish kids. A lot of issues that you disagree on may not be all that important to you both. The point is that one issue may be super important to one spouse and not to the other. Whenever that occurs, accede to the wishes of the one to whom the issue is most important.

5. Have boundaries/rules. Lorraine and I had friends who let their daughter hang out downtown as a 12-year-old. If her parents gave her rules, she routinely disobeyed them without consequences. Her parents forbad her to have a dog. She came home one day with a Great Dane puppy. The parents wound up caring for it. She never finished high school, and just got by working odd jobs or through the kindness of folks she met. If having rules that we enforced made us "strict" parents, I guess we were strict. We had rules, and there were consequences. Hopefully, we weren't unreasonable, and I recall times we modified or made exceptions to rules.

Once I was concerned that our son Ben was watching

too much television. Lorraine and I told him we were going to limit his time in front of the TV. Ben very calmly asked us why. He marshaled his facts and told us he was doing terrific in school (he was), was doing all of his homework, and was participating in extracurricular activities. Why was it then that we were going to limit his TV time? We didn't have a good answer, so we relented. By the way, Ben's a lawyer now. Go figure.

Zach loved soda as a boy. We limited him to one soda a day. One night he was at a birthday party, and he called us. He explained that there was soda at the party and asked if he could have a second one. We were thrilled that he asked us and didn't just try to have one behind our backs. We told him he could have a second one. We did the same with curfews. Subject to exceptions, the rules were enforced. Kids need limits. They're kids. Does anyone really believe a six-, 10- or 16-year-old truly knows what's best for them? That's why we don't let them decide what doctor to see, which foods to eat, or what school to attend. Beyond those obvious decisions, you can't let your child decide how late to stay up, whether to do schoolwork, or where they're going to hang out.

I know there were instances when rules were broken. Every soul should have a bit of rebellion. But our kids knew the rules and knew there were consequences when (if?) we learned they'd been broken. Sometimes I suppose the temptation to break the rules is just too great. When we had young sons, we didn't have the means to take expensive family vacations. That and the importance of visiting my folks in Wisconsin meant that we would take our summer vacations in Milwaukee. (Whenever we told people we were going to Milwaukee for our summer vacation, the inevitable response was "Oh, you have family there.") In the summer of 1990, after Jill graduated high school at 17, she stayed behind in Tucson when we left for our summer sojourn. While we were in Wisconsin, Jill called. "Mom, it's the weirdest thing, but I think someone came into our backyard and tried to steal one of our hedges." Huh?

Someone tried to steal one of the knee-high hedges that lined our back patio? "Jill, was it a hedge near the back gate, one at the end of the hedgerow?" "No, it was one right in the middle of the row." "Well," we told her, "we'll check it out when we get home."

Upon our arrival, we could see that no one had tried to steal a bush. We figured out pretty quickly that some drunk teenager had likely fallen on the bush and flattened it. You didn't need to be Sherlock Holmes to figure out Jill had thrown a party. The bush, the beer bottles strewn around the yard, the flat tire Lorraine got on one such broken beer bottle, and the neighbors saying, "Wow, that was some party you had last week" gave it away. Faced with overwhelming evidence, Jill confessed she had invited a "few friends" over, the word had spread, and the party had gotten out of control. Jill broke the rules. She was grounded.

To top it off, the real gravy on the sundae was that our phone bill contained a large charge to a sex hotline. Back in 1990, graphic sexual content was not yet available on the internet, most likely because there was no internet. Up until the internet, kids snuck a look at a *Playboy* magazine, *National Geographic* African tribe issue, or, worst-case scenario, a Sears catalog. A new innovation for these lonely hearts was the proliferation of 900- phone numbers that allowed you to make a late-night phone call, and for a meager $1.99 per minute, you could have someone talk dirty to you. I could've saved these folks a lot of money. Anyone who calls me after ten o'clock will hear me talk dirty to them. We eventually tracked down the call to the date when Jill had thrown the party.

Lorraine had an uncle named Donnie Catanzaro. Uncle Donnie told me a story about an incident when his daughters were little. One of them asked if she could go somewhere. Donnie told her no, and the girl responded, "I hate you." Donnie just looked at her and said, "That's okay. I'd rather you hate me today than me hate myself for the rest of my life." I never forgot that story.

6. Always be boyfriend and girlfriend. It's really easy to fall into the habit of being only Mom and Dad. It's really important for you and your spouse to continue to have a relationship separate and apart from being a parent. Kids don't like it. Often they'll cry or put up a fuss when you leave them with a sitter to go out for an evening, but it's important that you do. Seeing you as boyfriend and girlfriend gives them a model for what a healthy relationship looks like. When our kids were little, we had a babysitter named Tiffany. She was a busy student and worked part time providing daycare at a health club. One day, Tiffany asked us, "Is there an evening when you would like me to babysit?" Our response was succinct. "You let us know when you can come over. Whenever you can come, we'll leave."

This is not to suggest that there needs to be romance and fancy evenings out. It can be as simple as browsing a bookstore (should those still exist if and when someone reads this). It can be going out for a quick bite to eat, a cup of coffee, or a drink. But the two of you need to have a relationship. The children will not always be there. Or as I said in chapter 8 about life lesson I've learned, "it won't always be this way."

C HAPTER *22*

Would It Be Boring to Read about Your Law Practice?

Yes, it would. This will be a truly boring chapter for anyone other than a lawyer. Dreadful, really. On the bright side, this chapter will be a blessing for insomniacs who forgot to refill their Ambien prescription.

I had a pretty diverse and interesting law career. Among other cases, I represented criminal defendants, people whose home was taken by the state for a highway expansion, citizens who were wrongfully arrested, and homeowners who purchased defective houses. One common thread was that I represented people, not businesses. And while the Supreme Court in *Citizens United* ruled that corporations were people, my clients were real people who had a pulse. As a plaintiffs' attorney without a boss, I was able to pick and choose whom I wanted to represent. A defense attorney working for an insurance company has to defend every case the insurance company dumps on their desk.

After a dozen years of trying eminent domain, defective housing, police misconduct, wrongful discharge, and personal injury cases, I began to specialize in personal injury cases. I became a certified specialist by the Arizona State Bar in 1991, only the second year they offered such certification. However, I didn't want to do many traditional personal injury cases. Suing doctors for malpractice, manufacturers in products liability cases, or people in routine motor vehicle crashes didn't appeal to me. Every lawyer in the Yellow Pages seemed to be a personal injury lawyer. I really didn't know how to distinguish myself from the hundreds or even thousands of them, many of whom advertised.

Then in the mid-1990s, a young servicewoman stationed at Davis-Monthan Air Force Base was rendered a paraplegic as a result of a drunk-driving collision. She had attended a wine festival in Elgin, Arizona. The driver of her vehicle was to be the designated driver. However, he got drunk at the festival and was involved in a one-car collision when my client was his passenger. The law in Arizona had recently changed to allow dram shop cases, lawsuits against liquor licensees that overserved their customers. I successfully sued the wineries that were distributing wine at the festival, the festival organizers, and the Arizona Rangers, a group of uniformed citizens who had been hired to provide security and monitor alcohol consumption. In the course of that litigation, I became involved with Mothers Against Drunk Driving, MADD. Over time, I became involved in efforts to stop underage drinking, promote designated drivers, and educate bars and restaurants on their obligation to serve alcohol responsibly.

Over the last 30 years, I practiced law almost exclusively as a lawyer for crime victims in need of assistance in both criminal and civil cases. Without trying to sound noble, I felt that if I was going to represent someone in a personal injury case, I needed to also assist them as a victim representative in the criminal case.

When I began practicing law, victims had no rights in Arizona. The State of Arizona had an attorney to represent it. The defendants had an attorney to represent them. The victim couldn't have a lawyer. In fact, the victim had no rights at all. A criminal defense attorney could have them excluded from trial under the general rule that required witnesses to be excluded before they testified for fear their testimony would be influenced by the testimony of prior witnesses. Defense attorneys could interview a victim before the trial for as long as they wanted. Rape victims were often subjected to invasive, humiliating examinations. Victims had no input on a court's decision to release an accused prior to trial or a prosecutor's decision to offer a plea bargain. Things changed with the Victims Bill of Rights, which became part of the Arizona Constitution and was also codified in the Rules of Criminal Procedure. Victims could not be excluded from a criminal trial and had the right to refuse a pretrial interview by defense counsel. If requested, prosecutors were required to confer with victims before offering a plea bargain.

Representing crime victims required me to work with families that had suffered horrible tragedies. I was usually trying to hold a party or parties responsible for the death of a parent, spouse, or child. If you aren't a lawyer or particularly interested in litigation, this may be even more boring than the previous few paragraphs. Just a heads up because I'm going into the weeds on this.

Many states have enacted laws to limit the amount of compensation a victim can receive in damages. For example, some states have statutes that limit non-monetary damages to $250,000. Non-monetary damages are damages for your pain or your inability to enjoy activities of daily living, recreational activities, or intimacy. Monetary damages are hard numbers like medical bills, future medical bills, or lost income.

The gross unfairness of these limits is that people with minor injuries—a broken arm or leg—would be fully compensated for the few months they were unable to walk or play guitar. On the other hand, people with devastating life-changing injuries would not be fully compensated. Paraplegics could be awarded money for lost income and medical bills, but no more than $250,000 for having to be fed, dressed, bathed and unable to enjoy activities of daily living or intimacy for their entire lives.

I was fortunate to practice in Arizona where our constitution prohibits limiting damages. Additionally, for nearly my entire legal career, Arizona had strict comparative fault. What this meant is that anyone at fault paid a judgment only to the extent they were at fault. As an example, suppose a bar overserved a drunk driver, and the drunk then drove and killed someone. For simplicity, let's assume the jury awarded damages to the surviving widow in the sum of a million dollars.

The drunk driver would certainly be at fault for the harm that they caused, but the bar could also be at fault if they served alcohol to someone they knew or should have known to be intoxicated. The bar's knowledge that they were serving someone intoxicated could be based on the appearance of their customer or the amount of alcohol the person had been served. In that case, a jury could conclude that the drunk was 90 percent at fault and the bar bore 10 percent of the responsibility. In our example, the drunk driver would owe our widow $900,000, and the bar would owe $100,000. If you couldn't collect from the drunk because they had no assets or insurance, the victim was just out of luck for that part of the judgment.

(I told you I was going into the weeds here. Really, I'm not offended if you skip ahead to the next chapter. I'm getting drowsy writing this. But this explanation of Arizona's personal injury laws is important to understand my work representing crime victims.)

It was not uncommon for the parent of a child killed in a drunk-driving crash or other homicide to say, "It isn't right for me to make a profit over my dead child" or some similar refrain. I would explain that the responsible party is paying for the harm that they caused to them, not the harm they caused to their child. A jury is told that the surviving parent or widow is to be compensated for the loss they have suffered, the loneliness, the lack of companionship and love, not the harm to their deceased child.

I would explain to them that if the criminal had broken

their arm or cut off their leg, they would expect to be compensated for their injury. I would then ask them why the criminal should not have to compensate them for the far greater harm caused from having killed their child. The harm that the criminal had caused by taking their son or daughter was far worse than if the criminal had personally cut off their leg. Not infrequently, my clients used the compensation they received in a positive way to honor their child's memory. In one case, a client who had lost her son set up a scholarship in his name at a university. Another client had a bench installed at a beautiful Tucson hiking spot in memory of their son.

There were a few types of cases that I commonly accepted: dram shop cases, where someone had been overserved at a bar and then drove drunk, injuring or killing an innocent person; negligent security cases, where a bar or other business failed to exercise care to protect its patrons from foreseeable harm; and sexual assault cases. Let me explain my rules of the road for doing these cases.

For example, I never filed a civil lawsuit against a rapist while the criminal prosecution was pending. In a rape case, there are only two defenses: "I didn't do it" and, more commonly, "It was consensual." If I filed a civil lawsuit during the pendency of a criminal case, my action would undermine the victim's credibility in the criminal case. "Ms. Victim, you are suing my client for money, aren't you?" the criminal defense attorney would ask. In closing argument, the defense could then argue, "Of course she says it wasn't consensual. She can't get money from my client if she consented to sex. This is all about the money."

Additionally, in Arizona when a criminal defendant has been convicted in a criminal case, they can't deny the elements of the crime in a subsequent civil case seeking compensation for the harm caused. In other words, once convicted, they can't deny they raped the victim in a civil justice trial.

Finally, if you sue the rapist while the criminal case is pending, the attorney in the civil case can question the victim under oath in a deposition. If you recall from earlier in this chapter, under Arizona law a victim can refuse to be interviewed by a criminal defense attorney. However, when a civil case is filed, the victim can have her deposition taken and her sworn testimony will be given to the criminal defense attorney to use in her defense of a criminal case. (I say *her* because if you sue a man for raping a woman, smart defendants always hire a female lawyer to defend them at criminal and civil trials. Watch for this on television. If there's a case alleging racial discrimination, the defense attorney will usually be a person of color.)

Another rule was that because of comparative fault, there were many instances where it was in the victim's interest to try to place more or as much fault on someone other than the actual perpetrator. As I mentioned earlier, Arizona is a comparative fault jurisdiction. Consequently, if the drunk driver was uninsured or not adequately insured but the bar that overserved the drunk had sufficient assets or insurance, I would try to place as high a percentage of fault on the bar as the evidence established so that my client could be compensated as much as possible for their injuries.

Okay, so now I've gotten so deep into the weeds that any nonlawyer reading this is looking for a machete.

I could go on forever about the pitfalls and strategies for representing crime victims. I guess I already have. But I felt you needed this general background to understand what I did for most of my 42 years in practice.

While I did not win every case I took to trial, I won far more than I lost. Examples of the wide variety of cases I handled would take too long to recite, but I can provide some instances. I sued the Tucson Police Department on behalf of an African American woman who was wrongly arrested and taken away in handcuffs in front of her young daughter after a neighbor complained that she was making unreasonable noise. They were celebrating the life of a deceased relative in the early evening hours. Police arrested

My favorite office in an historic downtown Tucson building in May 2007

her despite hearing no noise when they arrived at her home.

I sued a school district when a young boy with special needs was disciplined by having to put on a girl's dress and a dunce cap and stand in front of the class. This was going to be the first time that the boy was going to have a male teacher, and his single mother had been excited that he would finally have a strong male role model. The defense counsel thought my case was "silly." He threatened to wear a dress during his closing argument. The jury didn't see it that way and awarded the child substantial compensation for the emotional harm that had been caused.

For a while, I represented employees who had been wrongfully terminated. Arizona was and is an at-will employment state, meaning that an employee could be fired for any reason or no reason as long as the termination was not based on a protected category like race. Until 1985, at-will employment was the law without exception. This meant an employee could be fired for attending jury service or refusing to engage in illegal activity.

I represented a man who worked for a moving company.

When a company truck overturned, he was asked to conceal from the customer that some of the items had been salvaged. When my client notified that customer that his employer had stolen the salvaged property, he was fired. The lower court dismissed my lawsuit because my client was an at-will employee. In 1985, the Arizona Court of Appeals reversed the trial court's decision, ruling that an exception to at-will employment existed if an employee was terminated for a purpose that violated public policy. *Vermillion AAA Pro Moving & Storage* is the case if you want to find it on the internet. After that Court of Appeals decision, the Arizona Supreme Court decided another case and reached the same result. Following the Supreme Court opinion, my case wasn't cited as precedent. Since that time the Arizona Legislature has addressed the issue of when a termination violates public policy by statute.

Many of my clients were women who had been sexually assaulted or had their privacy violated. There were several instances where a client had a good claim for which she could have been compensated but decided against pursuing it. Often after lengthy discussions with the client, we both concluded that reliving the assault and testifying against the assailant may not be in the best interest of her healing and her mental health. However, in cases where courageous women went forward and faced their accuser in court, my experience was that the victim felt empowered seeing her assailant looking small and powerless at the defense table.

I filed a lawsuit on behalf of a woman employed at a resort who was surreptitiously photographed in the women's restroom at work by an employee of another company that had been hired to videotape events at the resort. I sued a restaurant when a woman entered at closing for a takeout order. The drink she ordered while waiting for her food was likely spiked. While unconscious, she was repeatedly sexually assaulted by the manager of the restaurant after closing time on a floor of the establishment. Unbeknownst to the manager, surveillance cameras had filmed the assaults.

I represented a high school volleyball player when she was molested during a physical therapy session. Ironic that the word therapist can be broken into two words: *the rapist.*

Another interesting case concerned Artie Martinez, who spent nearly 40 years in the Arizona State Hospital for no reason other than that he was deaf. In 1955, Artie was arrested for disrobing in public and was sent to the Arizona State Hospital. Over the decades he spent institutionalized, Artie was completely isolated. No one at the hospital communicated in American Sign Language (ASL). Artie's sign language skills deteriorated. He not only lost his ability to communicate, but he also lost his teeth and any skills of independent living.

The law required that Artie's commitment be reviewed by a judge every year. Each year, a public defender would be appointed to accompany Artie to court, where he would appear disheveled and unable to communicate. Each year, a judge would conclude that Artie needed continued institutionalization. In the hospital, Artie often acted out in an attempt to be placed in solitary confinement so as to avoid abuse.

The Arizona Center for Law in the Public Interest learned of Artie's situation and argued that services he was entitled to were not being provided. Through their efforts, Artie was released from the state hospital in 1994. I don't recall how I became Artie's lawyer, but I assume it was because I had some ASL skills. In the early 1970s, I had a deaf friend named Tim Rice. Over the course of our friendship, including a cross-country drive from Maryland to Wisconsin; a weekend in his deaf dormitory at a vocational college for the deaf in St. Paul, Minnesota; and going to a silent club, I became somewhat competent at ASL. I was much better signing than reading sign language. When people signed to me, my response was usually signing the word *again* or *go slow* until they repeated themselves often enough or slow enough for me to comprehend.

I sued the State of Arizona for Artie's wrongful

institutionalization and for having violated his civil rights. Numerous defenses were raised, including the statute of limitations and the qualified immunity that the government enjoyed. The state argued that Arturo had been represented by competent counsel every year at his commitment hearing, that a judge had ruled he needed continued commitment to the hospital, and that if the judge had ruled incorrectly, Martinez should have appealed the ruling.

Arturo was born in 1926, and by the mid-1990s, he was already in his 70s. Protracted litigation was not in Arturo's best interest. I settled the case for low six figures. I believe it was $150,000, but the exact number escapes me. However, it was enough money for Artie to live in a group home, do artwork, and take fishing trips. The *Phoenix New Times* did a cover story about the case on October 2, 1997, titled "Deaf and Damned" if you're interested in learning more about it.

I was fortunate to be able to fight on behalf of the people on issues of my choosing. I enjoyed serving the community. When young lawyers ask me, "How do I market myself?" I tell them to get involved in the community on issues that they care about. It's a win-win. You'll become better known in the community and will likely raise your profile as an attorney. However, even if you don't get any cases or financial rewards for volunteering, you still help the community and become involved in areas of interest.

For example, I love jazz. I had the idea for a festival in 2014 and founded the Tucson Jazz Festival. I was concerned with police misconduct, so I was appointed to the Tucson Citizen Police Advisory Committee and became its first president from 1980 to 1981. Because of my work with crime victims for several years, I was the president of Homicide Survivors, Inc., a support and advocacy group for families that had suffered a devastating loss.

As a result of getting involved in organizations that matched my interests, I'm sure I got clients. But even if I'd never gotten a single case, I was proud of my work in the community. I served as the president of the Arizona

Association for Justice in 2013–2014 and on the advisory board of the National Crime Victims Bar Association. Occasionally, I was honored for my efforts. I received the AJC Learned Hand Award for Community Service for the State of Arizona in 2015, and the Steven M. Gootter Philanthropic Award in 2017. The Cystic Fibrosis Chapter of Tucson gave me the Breath of Life Award in 2009. Many of these awards were the result of the win-win situation of performing comedy to help nonprofit organizations and at the same time possibly raising my profile as an attorney.

CHAPTER 23

Why *So Far, So Good* for the Title?

A man fell out of a window on a building's hundredth floor. As he passed the 50th-floor window, an occupant looking out asked, "How's it going?" The man replied, "So far, so good." Now that's one positive attitude. Really in the moment and enjoying the view. That's the attitude I strive for, a moment-to-moment recognition of how fortunate I've been up to now. It's not that I view the world through rose-colored glasses, but I really have nothing to complain about. I'd be an ungrateful jerk if I didn't appreciate how good my life is and has always been.

"So far, so good" is an apt description of my life. "So far" because I've come a long way geographically, in my career, and my relationships. As a short, pimple-faced, eighth-grade failing student, I could never have imagined that I'd become a lawyer with a wonderful wife and children, that I'd do standup and sketch comedy for decades, that I'd start the Tucson Jazz Festival, and that I'd have a second home in Wisconsin (and Packer season tickets). I try to appreciate my unbelievably good fortune every day. If someday, like the falling man, everything comes to an abrupt *splat,* I'll do my best to be grateful for the trip.

While I've given them brief mention throughout this book, I'd be remiss if I didn't devote this final chapter to my family. You see, I wasn't always this appreciative. There was a time in my 40s when I hated being a lawyer. Despite making a more than adequate income to support my family, being in a contentious adversarial profession made me miserable. Being a trial lawyer meant that on every one of my cases, there was a lawyer on the other side doing everything in their power to beat me. Day and night, weekdays and weekends, it was difficult to shut off my mind from trying to anticipate their efforts. What objections could they make to prevent me from presenting evidence? What arguments could I make to prevent unfavorable evidence from being admitted? What would they argue, and what arguments could I make to be persuasive? How would I tell my client's story? What witnesses should testify first at trial to take advantage of the primacy effect? What witness should end my case?

Rather than being grateful, I was jealous of lawyers who weren't as smart, at least based on our law school grades, and didn't work as hard as I did but had a bigger income. I didn't sleep at night. When anyone asked how I felt about being a lawyer, my rote response was "I hate being a lawyer."

In my mid 40s, I looked into changing professions. I even hired a headhunter and began looking into my options, none of which paid nearly as well as my law practice. My wife, Lorraine, was 100 percent supportive. Never for a minute did she suggest that I needed to maintain my practice so we could continue to enjoy our lifestyle. Instead, she took pencil to paper to figure out how we could downsize so that I could be a schoolteacher or go back to school or whatever I decided to do. That's Lorraine. Practical. My wife has more common sense than almost anyone I know. She's sensitive not only to my feelings but to the feelings of others. I'm sure there may be better wives and mothers in the world, but I don't know any.

After looking at other options, I decided to stick with law. But I needed an attitude adjustment. I needed to be content with the terrific life I had, stop envying the success of others, and as best I as could, focus on the parts of my career that I enjoyed. I liked to brainstorm and strategize about cases. I enjoyed taking depositions, particularly of expert witnesses, where I'd need to educate myself about their field of expertise to effectively cross-examine them. I liked the camaraderie of working with other plaintiffs' lawyers. From that point forward, when someone asked, "Do you like being a lawyer?" I'd answer, "Yes. Yes, I enjoy my work." It was the beginning of the attitude adjustment. That's not to say I didn't have moments when I was down or that I never complained. My happiness and appreciation of my life became something I practiced, a never-ending work in progress.

Given the incredible kids Lorraine and I raised, how could I possibly not be grateful for my life? My daughter, Jill, is not related to me by blood. She has a dad, and she's not my daughter under the law. But she is without a doubt my daughter. If you haven't learned this already, family is whatever you make it to be. I know many brothers and sisters, fathers and mothers all sharing DNA who can't stand to be in the same room with each other. I know people who take in their son or daughter's friend, and they become a part of the family. I have the exact same love for Jill that I have for Ben and Zach. But it wasn't always easy.

When I started dating Lorraine, Jill was 10 years old. Her mom and dad had divorced. Lorraine had been engaged to a guy before meeting me. That ended too. Given those circumstances, it was no wonder Jill wasn't all that fond of the guy cutting in on her time with her mother and who would, in all likelihood, be on the scene only temporarily. She wasn't mean to me. She just wasn't particularly fond of me. So much so that at one point, Lorraine suggested we stop dating because Jill was such a pill. I told Lorraine that Jill wasn't about to scare me away. And with that, I wore her down. Jill, that is, not Lorraine. Okay, maybe Lorraine too.

Because of serious emotional/psychological illness, Jill's dad wasn't always present in her life. I taught Jill how to drive. (However, having driven with her, I think I should have sent her to Sears Driving School.) Lorraine and I took her to dance lessons and attended recitals. When she graduated high school, I helped her move into the dorm. My mom and dad called her their first granddaughter.

After only a month or two of college, Jill got a job as a dancer on Cunard cruise ships. The experience of being away from home for the better part of two years, both on the cruise ship and later living in New York, gave her a different perspective and greater appreciation for her mother and me. It took nine or 10 years, but Jill saw that I wasn't leaving, that I loved her mom, and that I loved her. Thirty years later, I'm so glad that Jill is part of my family. She and her husband, Josh Alpert, gave me the idea to write this book. Several years ago, Jill wrote the most beautiful piece telling me how much I meant to her and how important I had been in her life. You know, the kind of stuff a loving daughter does.

After some initial resistance, Jill became an incredible sister to her two younger brothers. There are 13 years between her and Ben and 15 years between Jill and Zach. Once we asked 16-year-old Jill to babysit her brothers when Lorraine and I wanted to go to a gym at 9 pm after three-year-old Ben and one-year-old Zach were asleep. "I never asked you to have kids" was Jill's response. Maybe she felt put upon or was jealous of the attention her brothers were getting, but any such feelings quickly passed. Jill was and still is the cool big sister. When rap music with lyrics inappropriate for small children was popular, Jill bought G-rated versions of rap CDs that were sold at Walmart. Undoubtedly, Zach at any age would have preferred the X-rated version of the CDs. On the other hand, once we told Ben that listening to inappropriate music wasn't allowed, he would never have listened. Probably still wouldn't.

From a young age, Ben followed rules—first rules that we imposed as his parents and then standards he put on himself. As a toddler, people commented that Ben had an old soul. From a young age, he wanted to learn. Before he was three, Ben could carry on lengthy discussions and tell you the name of every Major League Baseball team and the city where they played. Before he was verbal, I'd carry him through our house, and he would excitedly point at a light or an appliance and wait until I said the word *light* or *refrigerator*. He went to a Montessori school, and one of the aides was in a graduate program in psychology. Impressed with his intelligence and vocabulary, she asked if she could write a paper about him. I no longer know her name, but I can't help but think she wouldn't be surprised to learn that Ben grew up, was a straight-A student at Arizona State University Honors College, and attended Harvard Law School.

No one values family as much as Ben. When Jill needed a hip replacement and her husband, Josh, couldn't be there for a brief time during her recovery, Ben flew from Milwaukee to Portland to help his sister. Ben is also extremely generous. When the COVID-19 pandemic began, folks began working remotely and spent more time at home. A dog daycare service that Ben had used since his dog Archie was a puppy was struggling. With people staying home with their pets, no one was bringing their dogs to daycare. Ben gave the owner $5,000 dollars and told her that he'd have a credit for that amount when he once again began using her service.

Ben loves sports. He was a stringer for the *Arizona Daily Star* and the *Arizona Republic* in high school and college, covering high school sports. He currently does a podcast on Arizona State sports. His love of sports is probably only equaled by the passion of his brother, Zach.

Zach is one of the funniest people I know. He can go on a riff and get sustained belly laughs from an entire room. Ben is very funny. He can write comedy. Jill? Well, Jill's a terrific audience for her brothers. Zach is more of a performer. Always has been. When he was seven, Zach co-

The only formal family portrait the five originals ever had taken. I love it. Zach doesn't. He calls it the "Canadian tuxedo picture." I know the photographer liked it. It was displayed in his store window for years.

starred in a made-for-TV movie, *Seduced and Betrayed*. Zach had his own trailer and a director's chair with his name on it. He also was and is a terrific athlete.

Recently, he found an old journal that had very few entries. One entry was him beating me in a footrace. I remember that day too. Once your son beats you in any physical activity, you'll likely never win again. The only physical endeavor in which I have bested Zach or Ben recently has been a pushup contest. My secret is to always make them do pushups first so I know how many I have to beat. While he may not admit it, Zach is a truly sensitive soul. Like Jill and Ben, Zach is really smart. He's succeeded in every venture he's undertaken.

I'm proud of all my children. They all have graduate degrees. Ben has a law degree, and Zach has a master's in social work. Jill has a master's in social work and another in business administration. But that's not the main reason I'm proud of them. I'm proudest that they grew up to be kind, caring humans. I tell everyone that I'm the least nice person in my family. And I'm a nice guy. My kids' kindness is reflected in the good spouses they've chosen (or been chosen by?). They each married someone kind, smart, and passionate about others and about the planet.

Given all this, how can I not be appreciative and happy about life? Yeah, life changes. It won't always be like this. Sure, inevitably the *splat* will come. But so far, so good. So, so good.

Afterword

I began writing to jot down some comedy routines that I'd performed when I was younger, material that was no longer funny to perform at my age. I also shared a few hopefully humorous musings. However, the more I wrote, the clearer it became that I was revealing some personal information, sometimes exaggerated or embellished for comedic effect, but nonetheless very personal. At some point, I drifted into more truly biographical material, including the chapter about my 42-year legal career.

The Chapter on my work for crime victims became the longest in the book. While my work on behalf of victims was interesting and rewarding, I had some unease about my career. My compensation on every case was commensurate with the degree of suffering my client had endured. The more my client suffered, the greater the compensation I could obtain for them. The more compensation my client received, the larger my fee. A percentage of the compensation for a broken leg was far less than my fee when I represented a child whose parent has been killed by a drunk driver. I struggle a bit with the idea that my income was based on the misery of others.

Gail Leland's 14-year-old son was kidnapped from a chess tournament and murdered in 1981. The killer was never found. In the face of this unspeakable pain, Gail channeled her grief into action to help others facing the same unimaginable tragedy. Parents of Murdered Children, which later was renamed Homicide Survivors, Inc or HSI, was created to provide support and advocacy for grieving families. I confessed to Gail that I had some discomfort about making money from the pain of others. Gail looked me in the eye and said, "Elliot, prosecutors make money based on the pain of others. Funeral home directors and grief counselors are all in business because of terrible tragedies. When you get compensation for the survivors, you're helping them put their lives back together."

To balance the karmic scales, I volunteered on many groups. I served on the board of HSI, and for several years was its president. Our sons, Ben and Zach, attended Salpointe Catholic. While Ben attended, there was a troubling trend of a student, sometimes two, being killed in a drunk driving collision every year. While tragic, it seemed to many students, teachers and families that losing a classmate during high school was simply an inevitable part of growing up. Salpointe's principal formed a committee to try to change the culture called "Community of Concern". I was a founding member.

In 2008, Community of Concern began having evening presentations. One parent from every student's family was required to attend the program in order for their child to be able to attend Homecoming, Prom, etc. We had a psychiatrist tell parents about the effects of alcohol and drugs on the adolescent brain. I spoke about criminal and civil consequences for students and sometimes parents if their student injured or killed someone while drunk. Salpointe took the matter very seriously and over time began drug testing students and having a drug sniffing dog make unscheduled campus visits. As a result of these efforts, there were no student drug or alcohol related deaths for over 10 years.

Trying to establish that a bar had some fault in a drunk driving death was often challenging. In one case, I knew a drunk driver had been in a specific bar, but had no evidence as to how much alcohol he'd been served, or that he was served while he appeared intoxicated. Bar employees would never admit to overserving a customer. I went to the police department to review the jail inventory of items taken from the driver when he was arrested and taken to jail. A photo contained a dollar bill with a phone number on it. On a whim, I called the number. Based on this stroke of good fortune, I found a woman who had met the driver earlier that evening and given him her phone number. More importantly, she was able to testify that the bar was serving this gentleman when he was already obviously intoxicated.

In another case, a drunk driver killed someone after leaving a "Gentlemen's Club." Again, I didn't know how much alcohol he consumed or if he appeared intoxicated. However, I discovered the bar had surveillance videos of nearly all areas of the club. I was able to follow this customer from table to table and track how many drinks he was served and note the change in his appearance over the course of the night.

My involvement at Salpointe, even before Community of Concern, lead to my representation of an amazing woman and her family. On September 24, 2005, Donna McDermott had finished her shift at American Airlines in Tucson. She'd been working overtime for extra income. When she returned home, Donna's husband of over 20 years, Scott, suggested a quiet night at home. Scott and Donna rented a video from a nearby video store, and began the short drive home. At approximately 9:30 pm, with Donna driving and Scott in the passenger seat, they reached the four-way stop near Salpointe High School. After stopping and seeing no traffic, Donna proceeded into the intersection of this residential street. At that exact moment, 20-year-old Trevor Nelson blew past the stop sign and entered the intersection in his recently acquired Ford Mustang at over 75 miles per hour. The car struck the passenger door of Donna's car, instantly killing 51-year-old Scott McDermott. The initial belief of officers arriving at the scene was that Donna had also been killed.

Donna was alive and while her survival was thought

Donna and Scott McDermott

unlikely, Donna was taken to University Medical Center and admitted into the Intensive Care Unit. A priest from Salpointe was called to administer last rites. Organ donation personnel arrived to speak to Donna's family. Among Donna's injuries were "shearing brain injuries", a lumbar spine fracture, a fractured sacrum, fractured clavicle, a collapsed lung, fractured right humerus and multiple rib fractures. Donna was unconscious and breathing with a respirator.

Kyle and Sara, the 15-year-old son and 18-year-old daughter of the McDermotts, had been waiting at home for their parents return from the video store when they learned of the crash. Sara was a student at Pima Community College, Kyle a freshman at Salpointe. Scott's parents who lived just outside of Tucson and Donna's parents from the Chicago stepped in to care for the children.

Several attorneys were contacted by Donna's family that had flown to Tucson. Because of my work with Salpointe and Mothers Against Drunk Driving, I was contacted. Donna's brother-in-law interviewed me. After several discussions, Scott's parents, Donna's mom, dad and her siblings determined that I should represent Donna and her children to pursue civil justice.

There were multiple cases to pursue. Donna, her children and Scott's parents all had a claim for the loss they suffered as a result of Scott's death. Donna had a separate claim for her own injuries. In cases like these when there are limited funds from which to recover, a conflict of interest can arise. A lawyer cannot represent multiple claimants seeking to recover from the same limited funds unless the conflict of interest is resolved. The conflict exists because when there are limited funds available, a lawyer can't argue or decide that one client should get more money and another client less. I won't bore you with the details of how these conflicts can be resolved except to say all clients agreed on how sums would be allocated. Because there was a minor involved any distribution needed court approval.

Donna slowly recovered but had a long convalescence. Given the long term treatment she needed, Donna's family moved Donna to Chicago for physical therapy, speech therapy and occupational therapy while she lived with her parents. Donna could not manage her own affairs. She needed to relearn basic skills like walking and talking. Her brain injury impaired her cognition. Her daughter Sara was an adult and therefore able to make her own decisions on where to live. Kyle, her minor son, needed a guardian as he had no functioning parent in his life. Kyle was taken out of school, and moved to Chicago to live with his aunt and uncle. A conservator was appointed to handle Donna's finances.

In Arizona, an entity with a liquor license faced liability for serving alcohol to someone that was "obviously intoxicated" or someone they knew or had reason to know was impaired. In addition to lawsuits against bars and restaurants, I had cases against the Moose Lodge, a private club, a wine festival, and even a drive-through liquor store. As to the drive-thru liquor store, it was difficult finding evidence that alcohol was served to someone "obviously intoxicated". Since this isn't a treatise on how to prove fault, I won't go into detail on the evidence I garnered. I'll leave it to your own creativity to figure out how I proved a drive-through liquor store could be at fault when their customer never set foot out of his car and had only a brief interaction with the clerk.

Trevor Nelson, the underage driver that ran the stop sign and crashed into Donna McDermott's vehicle was uninsured. There was no automobile insurance from which to collect. While Donna had uninsured motorist coverage, it wasn't enough to begin to compensate the victims for the losses they sustained. Uninsured Motorist Coverage (UM) is insurance that people can buy to pay you in the event you are injured by an uninsured driver. It will pay up to the amount of UM motorist insurance coverage that the insured, in this case Donna McDermott, purchases. This coverage was grossly inadequate to cover the harm that Trevor Nelson caused. I investigated whether any other person or entity had some responsibility for this tragedy.

Nelson was not old enough to enter a bar and had been drinking at a private party of University of Arizona students. No tavern was to blame for serving the underage Nelson. Was anyone at fault from whom I could get compensation for Donna, her children and Scott's surviving parents?

In Arizona, a homeowner is not liable for any harm caused by someone of legal drinking age who gets drunk at their home and then injures someone while driving. If someone comes to my house, gets drunk on alcohol I serve, even if I know he's drunk, I'm not responsible for any harm he causes after he leaves my home. There is, however, an exception to this rule. If someone is under age of 21 and I provide alcohol to him, I'm responsible for the harm I've caused. Recalling the concept of comparative fault in a previous chapter, if a jury determined I bore 10 percent blame for a subsequent car crash because I served alcohol to the minor, I would be responsible for 10 percent of the damages.

Police reports revealed the identity of a passenger riding with Nelson. I filed suit against Nelson, his passenger who, according to the police, had contributed money for the purchase of alcohol at this underage drinking party. I also sued the person in whose home the party had taken place. In the course of taking depositions (questions and answers before a stenographer under oath), I learned the names of the university students that had pitched in to buy alcohol that Nelson had consumed.

I contacted each student and asked them to forward my correspondence to their parents' homeowners insurance company. A common misconception is that homeowner's insurance only pays for injuries that occur at your home, like someone tripping over a skateboard left in your driveway. In fact, homeowner's insurance covers all family members living in that household for negligent conduct. I've had cases where a family member took a shotgun to a wash and accidentally shot someone's eye out. Homeowners insurance covered that careless act. In another case, a person gave a young child access to a gun that was later used outside the home to accidentally shoot and kill someone. Homeowners insurance covered the negligent act of allowing a prohibited possessor access to a firearm.

The fact that the college students who chipped in for the alcohol that Nelson consumed were living far away from their parents did not mean they weren't covered by their parents' policy. Although homeowner's insurance only covers family members living in the home, if a child is away at college or in the military, the insurance covers them despite their temporarily being away.

One by one, I deposed the students, each one giving me the name of other students that had pitched in for the alcohol purchased for the party. By the end of the case, several students were identified as being at fault. Although each student may have had only a small percentage of fault, the harm that had been caused was so great that had they proceeded to fight the case, the total amount of the judgment even if they were only fractionally responsible could result in their having a judgment against them in excess of their insurance coverage. If a judgment is obtained in an amount greater that the insurance coverage, the student would be personally liable for the amount of the judgment not paid by their carrier. One by one, the insurance companies paid in order to protect their insureds from an "excess judgment". Even though the actual perpetrator had no insurance, I was able to obtain a significant recovery for Donna and her children.

Donna improved and over time she no longer needed a conservator. She and her son Kyle were able to return to Tucson. Donna never recovered the use of her right arm. She learned to eat and write and perform activities of daily living left-handed. Other than not using her right hand, someone meeting Donna would not notice any other deficits.

Sara became a tireless victims' advocate serving on the Board of Directors of Homicide Survivors, Inc. She moved to Colorado, got married and became very successful in the field of computer forensics. Shortly after writing this, I anticipate Kyle will have received a doctorate from the University of Washington.

Donna became involved with Mothers Against Drunk Driving. She also began speaking with me at Community of Concern at Salpointe High School. The policeman, the psychiatrist, and I were informative speakers when we spoke to parents about various problems caused by underage drinking but no one moved the audience more than Donna. People openly wept at her retelling of the events of September 24, 2005, and its aftermath. There is no way of knowing with certainty, but I'm confident as a result of Donna's talk, more than one parent didn't allow his son or daughter to attend an underage drinking party. In short, Donna's presentation saved lives. On an even happier note, after being widowed for over a decade, Donna found love for a second time.

Trevor Nelson was sentenced to prison. He began serving his sentence on May 4, 2007, and was released on March 3, 2014.

A few months ago, Lorraine and I had dinner with Donna, Kyle and Kyle's girlfriend. Kyle told me that he'd moved back to Tucson and was completing his doctorate from the University of Washington remotely. He then told me he'd purchased a home. I began telling him that homeownership was a great investment and that he could deduct the mortgage interest payments from his taxes. Kyle stopped me. "Elliot, I don't have a mortgage". "That's great", I replied, "How did you swing that?" Kyle looked me in the eye, smiled and said, "It's because of you, Elliot. It's because of you." I was taken aback. I'd never considered the impact the wrongful death settlement would have on Kyle's life. It was gratifying to observe an outcome that Gail Leland spoke of decades earlier.

For those of you wondering since Chapter 5, my final word count is 52,404 words!

Elliot Glicksman is a retired lawyer who, for most of his 42 year legal career worked to obtain compensation for crime victims, mostly people injured from a drunk driver or as the result of a sexual assault. He is the Past President of the Arizona Association for Justice and Homicide Survivors, Inc. He also served on the Advisory Board of the National Crime Victims Bar Association. Elliot was the also first President of the Tucson Citizen's Police Advisory Committee. He is also the founder and former President of the Tucson Jazz Festival.

For his community work, Elliot has been the recipient of the Arizona Chapter of the American Jewish Committee's 2014 Learned Hand Award for Community Service, the 2009 Cystic Fibrosis Breath of Life Award, a Compass Health Dynamic Duo Award with his wife Lorraine, the 2017 Steven M. Gootter Award for his philanthropic efforts, and in 2010 he was named one of the top 50 Pro Bono Lawyers in Arizona.

In 1981, Elliot began performing stand up comedy, first as one half of the team of Bob and Bob and later as Danny Boskowitz because he thought Elliot Glicksman might sound too Jewish. In the course of his comedy career, he opened for Jerry Seinfeld, Gilbert Gottfried and Phyllis Diller. Elliot is currently a member of Dave Fitzsimmons' Arroyo Café Players. Elliot is married to his wife Lorraine and is the father of Jill, Ben and Zach.

9 798986 404998